HISTORICAL ATLAS
OF DUBLIN

HISTORICAL ATLAS
OF DUBLIN

RICHARD KILLEEN

GILL & MACMILLAN

Gill & Macmillan Limited, Hume Avenue, Park West, Dublin 12, Ireland
and associated companies throughout the world.

ISBN Number   978 0 7171 4595 9

A CIP catalogue record for this book is available from the British Library.

Design and Cartography: Red Lion Media

Printed and bound in Malaysia

Typeset in Sabon and Trajan

5   4   3   2

For
Achala Siriwardhane

CONTENTS

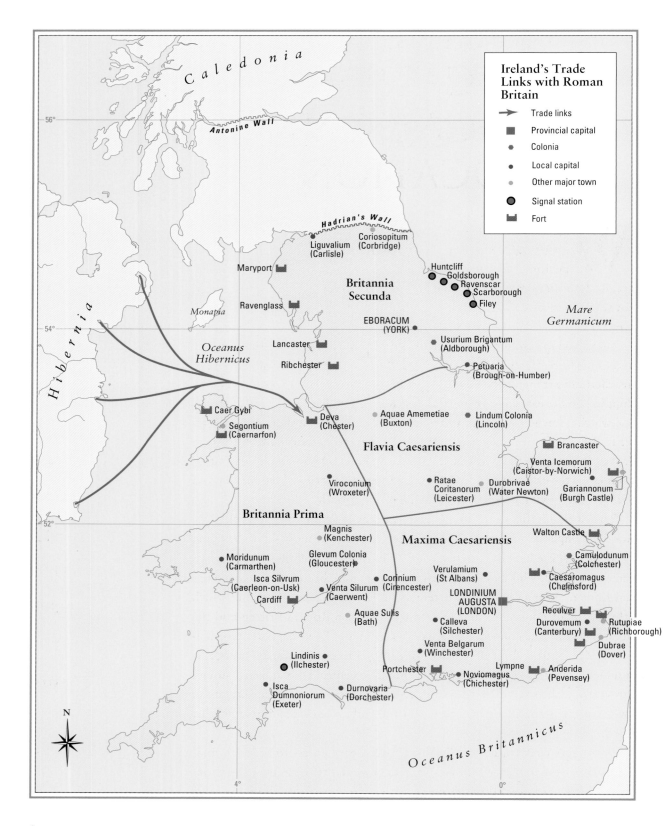

C a l e d o n i a

56°

Antonine Wall

Hadrian's Wall

Liguvalium
(Carlisle)

Coriosopitum
(Corbridge)

Maryport

**Britannia
Secunda**

Huntcliff
Goldsborough
Ravenscar
Scarborough
Filey

Monapia

Ravenglass

*Mare
Germanicus*

Hibernia

*Oceanus
Hibernicus*

54°

EBORACUM
(YORK)

Lancaster

Usurium Brigantum
(Aldborough)

Ribchester

Petuaria
(Brough-on-Humber)

Caer Gybi

Segontium
(Caernarfon)

Deva
(Chester)

Aquae Amemetiae
(Buxton)

Lindum Colonia
(Lincoln)

Flavia Caesariensis

Brancaster

Venta Icemorum
(Caistor-by-Norwich)

Viroconium
(Wroxeter)

Ratae
Coritanorum
(Leicester)

Durobrivae
(Water Newton)

Gariannonum
(Burgh Castle)

52°

Britannia Prima

Magnis
(Kenchester)

Glevum Colonia
(Gloucester)

Maxima Caesariensis

Walton Castle

Moridunum
(Carmarthen)

Corinium
(Cirencester)

Verulamium
(St Albans)

Camulodunum
(Colchester)

Isca Silvrum
(Caerleon-on-Usk)

Cardiff

Venta Silurum
(Caerwent)

Caesaromagus
(Chelmsford)

LONDINIUM
AUGUSTA
(LONDON)

Reculver

Aquae Sulis
(Bath)

Calleva
(Silchester)

Durovemum
(Canterbury)

Rutupiae
(Richborough)

Lindinis
(Ilchester)

Venta Belgarum
(Winchester)

Dubrae
(Dover)

Lympne

Anderida
(Pevensey)

Portchester

Noviomagus
(Chichester)

Isca
Dumnoniorum
(Exeter)

Durnovaria
(Dorchester)

N

Oceanus Britannicus

4°   0°

CHAPTER 1
LOCATION, LOCATION, LOCATION

Why is it where it is? It is a good question with which to start the history of any place. Was it a significant military and strategic position? Was it well located as a trading post? Was it on a natural harbour or at the tidal reach of a navigable river? Why is where it is and not somewhere else? Why did this particular place assume such significance over time?

Dublin wraps around a C-shaped bay, but it offers no natural deep-water harbour. The bay is shallow, tidal and possessed of a series of sandbars that are treacherous to shipping. None the less, the bay is the widest potential refuge for shipping on the east coast of Ireland. It is fed by a modest river, the Liffey, but one which is navigable at high water. It also commands the shortest sea crossing to Britain, if we exclude bays to the north like Carlingford and Belfast which deliver shipping to the wilds of the north of England and Scotland. Dublin commands the crossing to north Wales and to the estuaries of the Mersey and the Dee, thus giving access to the rich middle and south of England.

This was significant in Roman times, because at the mouth of the Dee stood the imperial outpost of Chester – for centuries the most significant port in north-west England. It is an historical commonplace that the Romans never came to Ireland. This is only a half-truth: there have been many archaeological finds of Roman coins and artefacts on the east coast of Ireland which offer proof of commerce and intercourse between Roman Britain and the smaller island. The connection between Chester and Dublin endured for centuries. The patron saint of Chester in early Christian times, Werburgh, is commemorated in a prominent parish church in central Dublin, just a stone's throw from Christ Church cathedral. As late as the 1720s, we find Jonathan Swift waiting impatiently at Chester for the Dublin packet ship to catch the tide to bring him home.

With one's back to the sea, Dublin afforded easy access to the Irish midlands. Due west along the Liffey valley and beyond, there are few natural obstacles to the progress of immigrants, settlers and invaders. While the same might be said of the mouth of the River Boyne, about forty kilometres to the north – whose valley holds the richest evidence of prehistoric settlement on the island – the river itself offers no harbour or bay to compare with Dublin. Further north again, Carlingford does offer a deep-water berthage but the landward access takes you into the hills and fastnesses which, for centuries, have girdled the province of Ulster and cut it off from the rest of the island. Pushing west from Dublin was a lot easier.

Even further north, the only significant harbour is at the mouth of the Lagan: Belfast. Its commerce, both human and material, was overwhelmingly with Scotland across the very short and equally treacherous North Channel, where the full force of the North Atlantic funnels through a passage less than twenty kilometres wide at the narrowest point. Historically, this region was part of the greater Gaelic seaborne kingdoms collectively known as Dal Riada, embracing east Ulster and Argyll. For centuries, the commerce across the North Channel was far more potent than any with the rest of the island of Ireland. Nor did the harbour induce a permanent settlement until early modern times: the city of Belfast dates only from the seventeenth century, whereas there is evidence of permanent settlement in Dublin a millennium earlier.

The only other location that might have challenged Dublin for primacy was Waterford at the south-east corner of the island, with its magnificent three-river estuary offering shipping an unrivalled safe haven. However, its most direct cross-channel passage carried you to west Wales, a region of stubborn remoteness, impervious over the centuries to settlement by Romans, Vikings, Normans, English and the rest of the world generally. Waterford was, in time, to develop into an important port but it never offered a serious challenge to Dublin for overall primacy.

Dublin offered a series of advantages, therefore, which in aggregate made it the most plausible location for a significant east-coast settlement. The origins of the first settlers are long lost to history but it appears that the landward side was as important as the seaward in this process. At Church Street bridge, a natural ford allowed passage across the river at low tide. From this point, a series of ancient roads penetrated to the interior. The ford itself was prone to inundation at spring tides and storms, so a sturdier artificial ford was constructed slightly upstream. This was the Ford of the Hurdles or, in Irish, Átha Cliath, from which the modern city takes its name in that language: Baile Átha Cliath, the town of the ford of the hurdles. These fords were a necessity, for the business of crossing the river was fraught with hazard. Over 700 members of a military raiding party are recorded as having drowned in the attempt in the eighth century.

Modern Dubliners are accustomed to the embanked river being contained

behind its quay walls from Heuston station to the sea. The embanking of the river began in Viking times, as the town gradually became a centre of trade and commerce, although for centuries the process was provisional, crude and haphazard. The modern appearance of the Liffey, flowing behind balustraded masonry quay walls, dates only from the eighteenth century. Prior to that – and most especially in pre-Viking days – the watercourse covered a much greater area than today. It is only possible to speculate on its exact course but there are clues, both archaeological and cartographical, that enable us to reconstruct it with reasonable confidence. The seventeenth-century maps of John Speed (1610: the first map of the town), de Gomme (1673) and Phillips (1685) all provide evidence of both the contemporary and historic situations.

On the north bank, the probable course of the river seems to have roughly followed the modern boundary as far east as the present Capel Street bridge, before gradually spreading to cover what is now the lower reaches of O'Connell Street. On the south side, however, a much more dramatic effect was created in what is now Parliament Street, the southern end of Temple Bar and the City Hall area. Here, a huge pool delivered the waters of the Poddle, a tributary whose course was later to wrap itself around the southern and eastern walls of

Howth Head forms the northern arm embracing Dublin Bay. This image shows the southern shore and the Wicklow Mountains in the distance. All seaborne immigrants to Dublin would have sailed under the shadow of Howth Head.

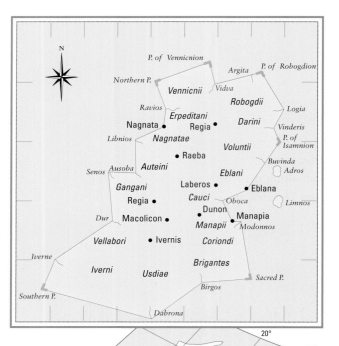

Ptolemy's Map c. AD 100

Promontory   River mouth   *Iverni* Tribe   • City

Dublin Castle, into the Liffey. All the modern streets and places mentioned stand on land reclaimed from this triangular Poddle pool. The dark waters of this pool bore the Irish name Dubh Linn, which in time came to denote the whole district to the east of the Poddle confluence, while the area to the west retained the older name of Átha Cliath. The eastern settle-

Below: *Part of the Greek geographer's map of the world by Claudius Ptolemaeus (Ptolemy). It shows Ireland (Juvernia) on the far north-western edge of the Roman Empire. The enlargement* (upper left) *is based on detailed co-ordinates from Ptolemy's Geography. It shows the position of Ireland's main tribes and towns.*

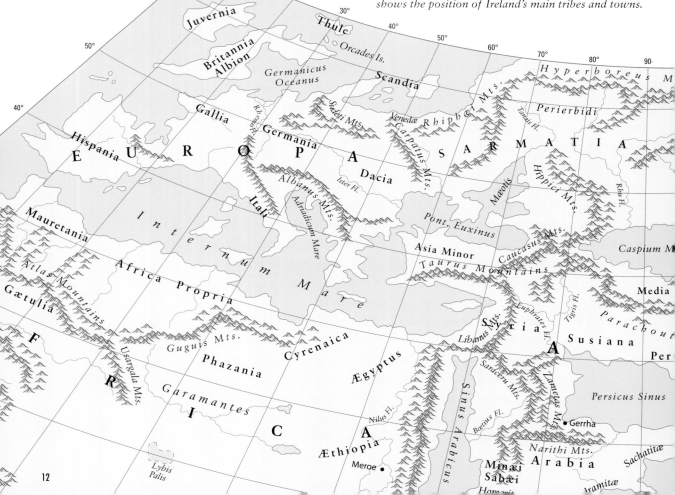

ment was principally the site of religious houses, the older, western one was mainly secular in purpose. Of the two Irish-language names, it was Dubh Linn that was eventually anglicised to giver the city its name.

As for the Poddle, its pool was gradually reclaimed in the course of the seventeenth century and it was finally culverted in the eighteenth. It may now be seen issuing into the Liffey from its exit in the quay wall just below the Clarence Hotel. In *Ulysses*, set in 1904, Joyce records the entourage of the lord lieutenant ("William Humble, Earl of Dudley, and Lady Dudley, accompanied by lieutenant-colonel Heseltine") making its ceremonial way along the north quays while "from its sluice in Wood Quay wall under Tom Devan's office Poddle river hung out in fealty a tongue of liquid sewage".

There was evidence of settlement around the bay from Mesolithic times, more so from the later Neolithic period. Still, this takes us back to about 4000 BC. The Celts, who first irrupt into Ireland around 250 BC, also appear to have had some sort of settlement on the rising ground above the ford close to Christ Church. This was the obvious location for settlement, being contiguous to the ford – and therefore to the system of roads and trading routes previously noted – and reasonably easily defensible. It is no accident that this area became the locus of the Viking and Norman towns and of Dublin Castle.

Pre-Viking Dublin, therefore, had a vestigial but palpable existence. It stood at the junction of an internal road system that reached into the heart of the island; it presumably had some sort of primitive trading function, both internal and with Roman Britain, and it was the principal port of entry to and departure from the east coast of Ireland. All of this can be asserted with reasonable confidence, although there is no historical evidence in the modern sense to support it.

Well, almost none. Ptolemy's map of the second century CE shows Ireland as a triangular shaped island to the west of Britain, with a settlement about half way along the east coast called Eblana. It has been suggested that this is the earliest cartographical acknowledgment of the presence of what later became Dublin. Further, it must have been in existence for some time in order to be known to Ptolemy. There has been a great deal of scholarly dispute about this claim. It is enough to acknowledge here that the matter can never be resolved definitively, but that there most likely was a settlement of sufficient significance in this region to come to the notice of Ptolemy in faraway Alexandria. On the logic of the discussion above, any such settlement was most likely to have been found around the shores of Dublin Bay.

Whatever its nature, the settlement never developed the sinews of a town in any sense that modern people could acknowledge. That had to await the arrival of the Vikings, with whom the history of the city proper may be said to begin.

Bulloch

Bulloch Harbour lies on the south-east of the bay between Dun Laoghaire and Dalkey. It was one of a number of landing points and safe havens in the outer bay to which shipping had recourse because of the navigation difficulties in the main river channel, caused principally but not exclusively by the harbour bar.

The bar lies to the east of the river mouth at Poolbeg. It is a sandbar running roughly from the Bull Island (formerly the North Bull sandbank) to Sandymount strand (formerly the South Bull). At low tide, and especially in rough weather, the bar reduced the draught available to shipping – even to shallow-draughted vessels – to a dangerous minimum. There was therefore an incentive to find safe landing points or havens at other points in the bay. Bulloch Harbour was one such. The added cost of ferrying cargoes and passengers into Dublin was deemed worth it in the circumstances.

On the north shore of the bay, Sutton Creek afforded no similar landing place but it did offer a haven in which shipping could take shelter in storms. Within the bar itself, once shipping had negotiated it, the problem of finding safe landing places was not finally resolved until the building of the Great South Wall and the Bull Wall in the eighteenth and nineteenth centuries. Prior to that, and to the full embankment of the river, it was often impossible to proceed any further towards the city than Ringsend.

Ringsend stands at the confluence of the Liffey and the Dodder, its principal tributary to the south-east of the city. The lesser river formed a spit of land at its end which remained high and dry at all times and was a recognised landing stage for goods and passengers alike from at least the fourteenth century. A defensive fortification stood here from early days and Cromwell landed his troops, most of them wretched with seasickness, at Ringsend in 1649.

The necessity for landing places and safe havens was a problem that has affected the bay until modern times. The estuary port did not develop fully until the nineteenth and twentieth centuries, and consequently the main river was unsuitable for the mail package boats when they started to ply between Britain and Ireland as early as the late sixteenth century. Liverpool, Chester and Holyhead (from 1576) all served the Irish capital, carrying both mail and passengers.

Up to the start of the nineteenth century, the packet boats generally unloaded cargo and people either at Ringsend or even further down river near the Pigeon House. Neither of these locations was satisfactory for the purpose. In 1807, it was decided to move the landing point for packet boats to Howth, on the northern extremity of the bay. A harbour was duly constructed and service began in 1818.

It was not a success. The harbour was small, which became an insuperable problem with the arrival of steamships on the service, and silting was a constant nuisance. In 1833, the decision was taken to move the service across the bay to Kingstown (now Dún Laoghaire), from which it still operates.

These several expedients, covering the entire range of Dublin Bay and the full sweep of its history, demonstrate the difficulties presented at the mouth of the Liffey. And yet, for all these difficulties and the vexations involved in circumventing them, it was on the river that the city of Dublin developed and grew.

Dublin Bay looking north, with Dun Laoghaire harbour in the middle ground.

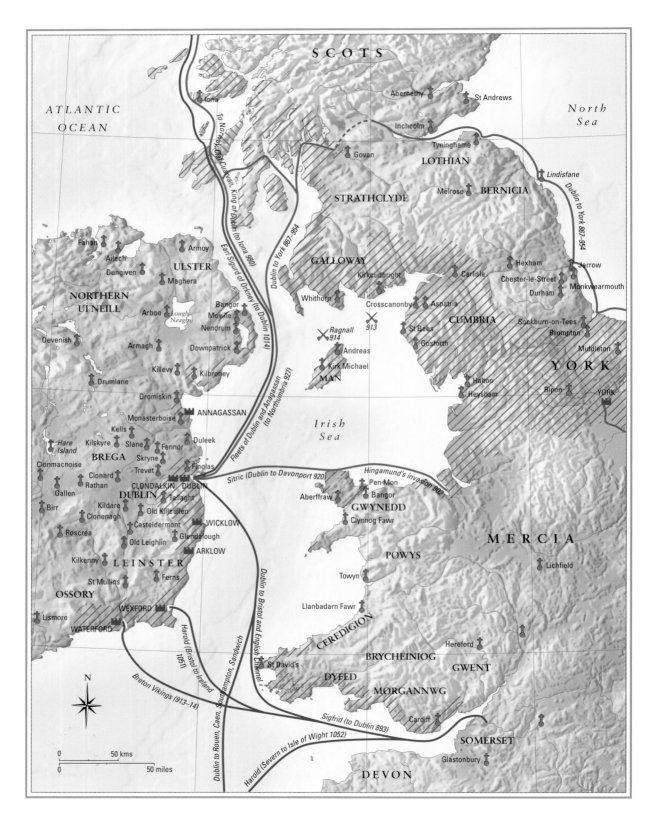

CHAPTER 2
VIKINGS

With the Vikings, we move from prehistory to history. All the prehistoric "evidence" is inferential, depending upon archaeological probability. Once we enter the Viking era, we have written records. There is nothing infallible about the written word, but it does give us greater certainty about the course of events. This is especially so if we can compare records from opposing sides of a conflict or from contending points of view. For all the doubts that may be expressed from time to time about written sources – history being written by the winners and all that – such sources are indispensible.

The term Viking refers to groups of Scandinavian people principally from the south and west coasts of what is now Norway, and the Jutland peninsula to the south across the Skagerrak. These people, in possession of their lands from ancient times, had probably been part of successive patterns of migration by Germanic tribes across the Great Northern Plain of Europe, which offered few natural obstacles to such migration.

Quite what impelled the Vikings to their sudden, violent and energetic expansion overseas from the eighth century CE is uncertain. There may have been population pressures, which would have been particularly severe in Norway with its rocky coastal valleys trapped and surrounded by impassable mountains on the landward side. The combination of limited and poor land together with the unforgiving northern climate would have made such habitats especially vulnerable to population growth, with any surplus population impelled to shift for itself. The gradual development of the proto-kingdoms of Norway and Denmark in the early Viking period may also have caused tribal groups alienated from the move towards centralised kingdoms to seek their fortunes elsewhere.

Whatever the reasons, the facts are incontrovertible. The Vikings developed the finest fleet of seafaring craft in contemporary Europe, which carried them to Britain and Ireland, north-west France, and as far east as Novgorod in Russia. The first Viking raid on Britain occurred in 789, but the most dramatic early assault was on the holy island and monastery of Lindisfarne in Northumbria. Lindisfarne was one of the great jewels of the Columban

An exquisite silver chalace with gilt bronze decorations, was made around AD 700. It was part of a hoard of valuables buried during the Viking Age and was unearthed in 1868 at Ardagh, County Limerick.

Dublin's Trade Network in the Viking Age 800–1170

- ◪ Areas colonised by the Norse
- ▬ Major routes, 9th–10th centuries
- ▬ Major routes, 11th–12th centuries
- ♜ Scandinavian fortresses
- ♄ Ecclesiastical centres
- ✕ Battle sites with dates

church and was originally of Gaelic Irish foundation. Its founder, St Aidan, had been sent from Iona to evangelise the north of England. Like all the great monasteries, it was not simply a centre of piety and prayer but also of scholarship, ritual and high artistic achievement. Its finest accomplishment, almost a century old at the time of the first Viking raid, was the Lindisfarne Gospels, one of the greatest treasures from the golden age of illuminated gospel manuscripts.

The *Anglo-Saxon Chronicle* records the shock of the Viking raid: "In this year fierce, foreboding omens came over the land of Northumbria. There were excessive whirlwinds, lightning storms, and fiery dragons were seen flying in the sky. These signs were followed by great famine, and on January 8th the ravaging of heathen men destroyed God's church at Lindisfarne." Alcuin of York (c. 737–804), perhaps the most influential English monk of the period and a leading official at the court of the Emperor Charlemagne, observed: "Never before has such terror appeared in Britain as we have now suffered from a pagan race. … The heathens poured out the blood of saints around the altar, and trampled on the bodies of saints in the temple of God, like dung in the streets."

Reconstructed Viking-Age trading ships. The Vikings developed specialist merchant ships to meet their needs. On the right a small coasting vessel and on the left a deep-sea trader or Knarr.

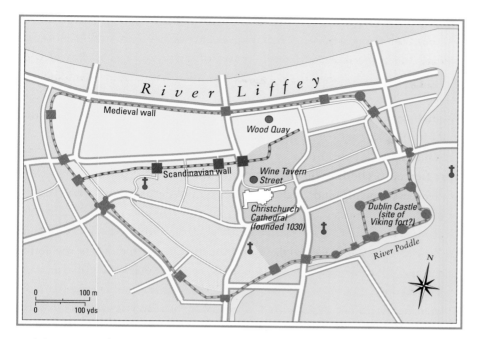

Two years after Lindisfarne, in 795, the Vikings appear for the first time off the Irish coast and attacked the wealthy monastery on Lambay island, just north of Dublin Bay. They were raiding in search of loot and treasure and in this they were not alone, for native Irish raiders did not scruple to emulate their example. Undefended monasteries and their riches made a tempting target. For almost half a century, these Viking depredations continued with the Norse the principal presence on the east and south coasts while the Danes pushed farther inland in their shallow-draughted longboats.

This so-called "hit and run" period ended in 841 with the establishment of a proto-settlement, known as a longphort, on the banks of the Liffey. A longphort was a defensible enclosure for shipping which offered adequate berthage and easy access to the open sea. The establishment of the settlement marks the foundation date of the city of Dublin. The towns of Cork, Limerick, Wexford and Waterford all followed before 900, all of them of Viking foundation.

The longphort was not a town, although a town was to grow from it. Its purpose was to give shelter. Shelter suggested some degree of permanence, if only in the winter months. Permanence suggested continuity; the domestication of skills; trade and commerce. The Vikings had established secure control of the sea lanes all around the larger island of Britain, including staging posts in places like the Isle of Man. In 866 they established themselves in the old Roman city of York, from where they controlled the first Norse kingdom in the north of England. In short, Dublin became a link in a chain of Viking trading centres, joined by their secure control of the sea.

Dublin, Ireland's first true town, originated as a 'longphort', a fortified enclosure built by the Vikings in 841 to protect their ships and act as a raiding base. Dublin probably developed as centre for slave trading and excavations have shown that, by the 10th century, it had become a prosperous merchant and manufacturing town.

The Dublin longphort lasted until 902, when the native Irish drove the Vikings out. Quite what that bald statement means is unclear, because the settlement had been under pressure from the beginning. The Vikings did not win all their battles with the Irish. On the other hand, there is evidence of inter-marriage and social intercourse from the earliest days, of linguistic confusion and melding, and of ad hoc military and other alliances both formal and informal. It has been speculated – there is no firm evidence – that the expulsion of the Vikings in 902 only affected the military leadership and that domestic tradesmen and such like remained behind.

What is clear is that Viking power on the banks of the Liffey was broken until 917, when the leading families returned from their English exile. In England, where urban settlement and development was more advanced than in Ireland, they would have seen towns that were sophisticated by the standards of the age. They brought this knowledge back to Dublin. From this point on, it is customary to refer to the Viking city's dún phase, from the Gaelic word for fortification. No longer merely a longphort, the town now had an early, permanent stockade within which the community could find security. That security was not absolute: there were Gaelic incursions throughout the tenth century. The settlement was burned down in 936 but Norse power was subsequently reasserted and the little town rebuilt.

Throughout the tenth century, control of the town remained for the most part in Viking hands, although there were interludes of Gaelic success and the town passed into Irish hands for at least one short period towards the end of the century. From Dublin, the Vikings were able to raid inland but it was their commerce across the Irish Sea – by now a Viking lake – that gave the town its raison d'être.

The commerce of Viking Dublin entailed trade with the Isle of Man and with Viking centres in Britain such as York. The slave trade was a significant feature of both its imports and exports which also included animal hides, wool and jewellery. The stability of commerce found expression in the development of the urban infrastructure. The ever-increasing pressure from the Irish kings and warlords from the 980s onward was a problem, but also provided an opportunity. For as long as the battle for control was inconclusive, provisional arrangements and compromises in the form of inter-marriage alliances gave the town an increasingly mixed ethnic character. This in turn led to linguistic ambiguity, as Norse and Gaelic borrowed from each other and a hybrid form developed.

However, the pressure from the Gaelic world was persistent and ultimately proved decisive. From around 1000 CE, Viking power in the town was fatally compromised. In part, this was due to the rise of Brian Boru as a true high

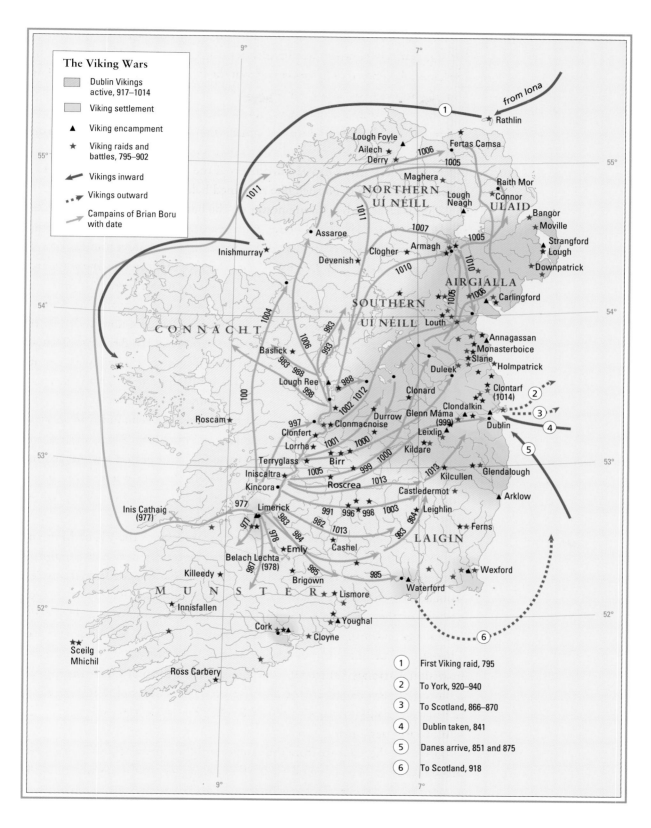

The Viking Wars

- Dublin Vikings active, 917–1014
- Viking settlement
- ▲ Viking encampment
- ★ Viking raids and battles, 795–902
- → Vikings inward
- ⇢ Vikings outward
- → Campains of Brian Boru with date

from Iona

★ Rathlin

Lough Foyle
Ailech ★
Derry ★   1006
Fertas Camsa ★   1005

Maghera ★
Raith Mor ★
NORTHERN
UÍ NÉILL
Lough Neagh
Connor ★
ULAID

Bangor ★
Moville ★
Assaroe ●
Strangford ▲ Lough ★
Clogher ★   1007
Armagh ★   1005
Downpatrick ★

Devenish ★
1010
AIRGIALLA

Inishmurray ★

CONNACHT
SOUTHERN
UÍ NÉILL
1005 1006
Carlingford ▲
1004
Louth ★

983
Annagassan ★
Baslick ★
Monasterboice ★
993
983 988
988
Duleek ●
Slane ★
Holmpatrick ★
Lough Ree
998
Clonard ●

Roscam ★
1002 1012
Durrow ●
Glenn Máma
(999)
Clontarf (1014)

997
Clonmacnoise ★
Glenn Máma ★
Clondalkin ▲

Clonfert ★
1001
1000
Kildare ★
Leixlip ▲
Dublin ▲
Lorrha ★
Birr ★
999 1000

Terryglass ★
1005
Roscrea ★   1013
Kilcullen ★
Glendalough ★

Iniscaltra ★
Castledermot ★
Kincora ●
991 996 998 1003
Arklow ▲

Inis Cathaig
(977)
Limerick
984 Leighlin ★
983
Ferns ★★
977
982
1013
Emly ★
978 984
Cashel ★
985 LAIGIN

Belach Lechta
(978)
985
Wexford ★★
Killeedy ★
Brigown ★
Waterford ▲

MUNSTER
Lismore ★
★ Innisfallen

Youghal ▲
Cork ●▲
Cloyne ★

★★
Sceilg
Mhichil

Ross Carbery ★

① First Viking raid, 795

② To York, 920–940

③ To Scotland, 866–870

④ Dublin taken, 841

⑤ Danes arrive, 851 and 875

⑥ To Scotland, 918

king of a united Gaelic polity, providing for the first time in the island's history a more or less central political and military authority. Brian is the only leader of Gaelic Ireland to whom the term high king – one of the most abused shibboleths in Irish history – may plausibly be ascribed.

Even then, Brian's centralising impulse met with resistance from provincial sub-kings and their princely underlings. In order to deal with them, Brian was content to permit Viking Dublin a continuing degree of local autonomy. However, the king of Leinster, Máel Mórdha, outbid Brian with promises of autonomy to Dublin and succeeded in enlisting the support of the Viking ruler, Sitric Silkenbeard, in a provincial revolt against the power of the high king.

The issue was joined at Clontarf, on the north shores of Dublin Bay, on Good Friday 1014. The Dublin Norse and their Leinster allies were augmented by Viking troops from Britain, Norway, Denmark and the Isle of Man. Against them was ranged Brian's coalition principally comprising troops from Munster, Connacht and the midlands.

The Battle of Clontarf, one of the most famous fights in Irish history, is a misnomer. It did not take place on land now occupied by the modern suburb of that name, but most likely to the west of it in the general area of modern Ballybough. In fact, for those familiar with prominent landmarks in the modern city, the most plausible location for the main battle is in the general vicinity of Croke Park, the city's biggest sports stadium.

Brian won, although the battle cost him his life as well as that of his son and fifteen-year-old grandson. This is important given the context of the battle. It is usually celebrated as the moment that Ireland was rid of the Viking yoke. This is an exaggeration. Norse power was undoubtedly weakened: they had backed the losing side in a major battle but Sitric remained the ruler of the town until his death in 1036. Vikings then retained the leadership of Dublin until at least 1042 and remained a significant presence until the arrival of the Normans over a century later. Even more significant was the failure of the Irish kings to deepen the centralising process that Brian had established in arms. His successors were unable to emulate him, leaving Gaelic Ireland politically divided and vulnerable to the next major invasion from a more sophisticated military society.

The effective assimilation of the Vikings was complete with their embrace of Christianity in the years after Clontarf. However, in a development that was to be hugely significant in the next century, they refused to accept the authority of the see of Armagh – the primatial Irish see – but placed themselves under the protection of Canterbury instead. This status was challenged at the Synod of Kells in 1152, which created the archdioceses of Dublin and

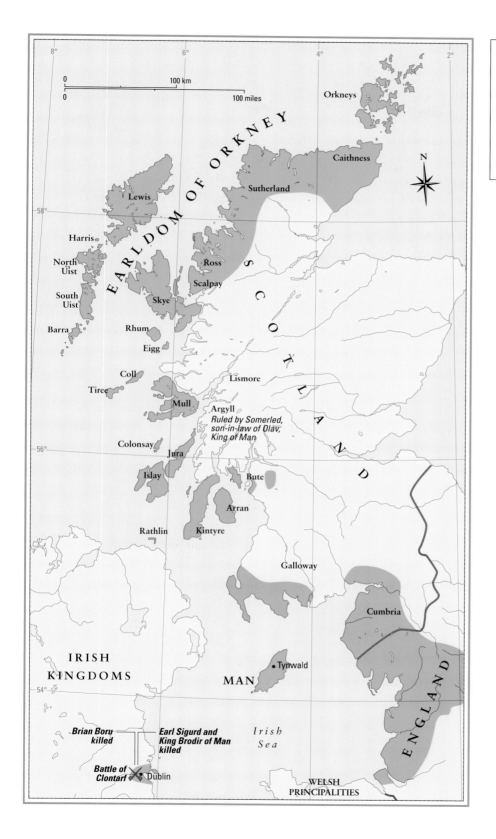

Viking Lands in the British Isles
c. 1014

Lands under Viking control

Land settled by Vikings, nominallly under the control of English or Scottish kings

0 — 100 km
0 — 100 miles

N

Orkneys

Caithness

Sutherland

EARLDOM OF ORKNEY

Lewis

Harris

North Uist

Ross

South Uist

Scalpay

Skye

Barra

Rhum

Eigg

Coll

Tiree

S C O T L A N D

Lismore

Mull

Argyll
Ruled by Somerled, son-in-law of Olav, King of Man

Colonsay

Jura

Islay

Bute

Arran

Rathlin

Kintyre

Galloway

Cumbria

IRISH

KINGDOMS

MAN

Tynwald

E N G L A N D

Irish Sea

Brian Boru killed

Earl Sigurd and King Brodir of Man killed

Battle of Clontarf ⚔ Dublin

WELSH PRINCIPALITIES

Tuam to join the existing archepiscopal sees of Cashel and Armagh. It meant that the ecclesiastical status of Dublin was contested.

Christ Church cathedral dates from 1038. It stood, as its successor stands today, on the southern lip of the ridge that rises from the river and that runs from west to east – from modern Kilmainham to College Green – along which ran the main thoroughfare of the town. An earlier church, that of St Olaf, stood on what is now nearby Fishamble Street. It is named for Olaf Haraldsson, a Christian King of Norway who was canonised shortly after his death.

Across the river, the church of St Michan dates from 1095 and formed the focus of a small suburban settlement. It was joined to the main town by a permanent bridge where Fr Mathew bridge now stands. For 600 years, it remained the only parish church on the north bank of the river, but it became the focus of a series of religious settlements. A monastery dating from 1139 later became part of the Cistercian foundation known as St Mary's Abbey.

The most dramatic urban development of the so-called Hiberno-Norse period in the town's history – from 1014 to 1170 – was the construction of the city walls. Hitherto, the various defensive enclosures and stockades had been constructed of earthen banks with timber reinforcements. But from the late eleventh century, the entire urban area was protected by a continuous stone wall, one of the very few contemporary towns in north-west Europe to be so defended. The walled area enclosed a space roughly bounded by Parliament Street, Essex Street East, Cook Street and then arcing back to the Castle in a loop that embraced Christ Church but excluded the site of what would later be St Patrick's cathedral.

St Audeon's Arch and another small section of the Hiberno-Norse wall are still extant between Cornmarket and Cook Street, although they suffered from Victorian "restoration" techniques in the late nineteenth century which have changed their original character. The alternative had been outright demolition, the preferred option of the Corporation which was restrained only by public protest.

In many respects, the history of the city has been its expansion beyond these walls. This happened gradually in all directions over time, but the key direction was east, towards the bay. Over centuries, the city's centre of gravity moved east from the Christ Church area towards College Green and O'Connell Street, a pattern that is being repeated in our own time by the development of the docklands along the north and south quays.

A crucial moment in this eastward drift came in the 1160s with the foundation the Augustinian priory of All Hallows at a site called Hoggen Green, now College Green. The site on which the priory stood – it was closed at the dissolution of the monasteries under Henry VIII – is now occupied by Trin-

Archaeology has revealed Dublin's Viking past. This is the floor plan of a house on the Fishamble Street–Wood Quay site which was excavated prior to the building of the Civic Offices in the early 1980s.

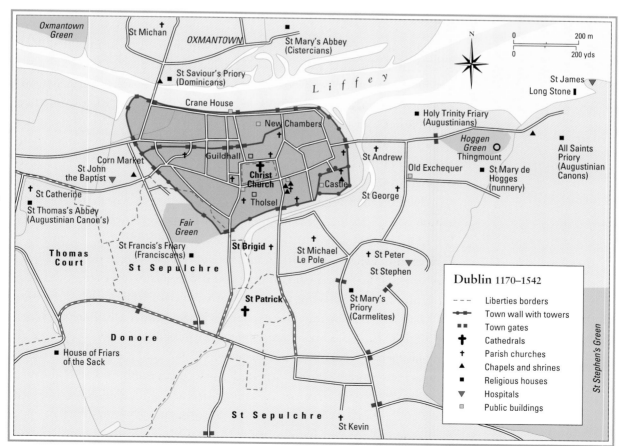

Oxmantown Green

St Michan

OXMANTOWN

St Mary's Abbey (Cistercians)

St Saviour's Priory (Dominicans)

N

0 ——— 200 m
0 ——— 200 yds

L i f f e y

St James
Long Stone

Crane House

Holy Trinity Friary (Augustinians)

New Chambers

Hoggen Green
Thingmount

All Saints Priory (Augustinian Canons)

Corn Market
St John the Baptist

Guildhall

St Andrew

St Catherine

Christ Church

Old Exchequer

St Mary de Hogges (nunnery)

St Thomas's Abbey (Augustinian Canon's)

Tholsel

Castle

St George

Fair Green

Thomas Court

St Francis's Friary (Franciscans)

St Brigid

St Michael Le Pole

St George

St Peter
St Stephen

St Sepulchre

Donore

House of Friars of the Sack

St Patrick

St Mary's Priory (Carmelites)

St Stephen's Green

Dublin 1170–1542

- – – – Liberties borders
- ●▬● Town wall with towers
- ▪▪ Town gates
- ✝ Cathedrals
- ✝ Parish churches
- ▲ Chapels and shrines
- ■ Religious houses
- ▼ Hospitals
- □ Public buildings

St Sepulchre

St Kevin

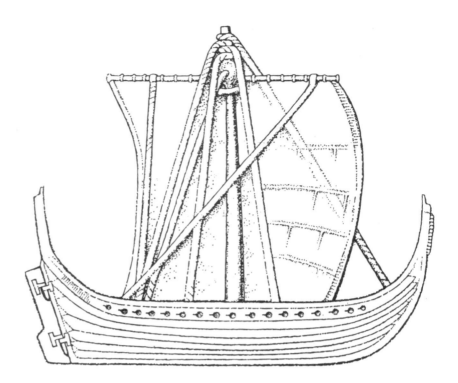

This illustration based, on a carving on a tomb dating from the 1500s, shows a Nyvaig. The Nyvaig sailed the Hebridean Islands and the Irish Sea and occasionally far beyond. Its Scandinavian influence can clearly be seen. The steering oar has now been replaced by a much more effective stern rudder.

ity College. Nearby, on the site of the former St Andrew's church (now the main Dublin Tourist Office), the king of Leinster, Diarmait Mac Murchada, had endowed the convent of St Mary de Hogges in 1146. The provision of green areas for commonage and grazing was an important part of the town's extra-mural development. Horses and cattle were required for draught purposes and as a source of food, so grazing areas were a crucial part of the town's supply chain of essentials. The best known modern green – St Stephen's Green – started life in a similar way.

The drift eastwards was not to reach its full flowering until the Georgian era, with the development of Merrion and Fitzwilliam Squares and later by the further development of the inner south-east suburbs in the Victorian era, thus giving us the postal district and state of mind known today as Dublin 4. But it is significant that even as early as the Hiberno-Norse period, the drang nach osten was already the most notable aspect of Dublin's early expansion.

There was also a westward expansion beyond the walls along the line of what is now Thomas Street and immediately north and south of it, from the river into what later became the Liberties. But this area was never fashionable, nor was it a centre of power. It remains one of the poorer parts of the modern city. Power and influence tended east, following the progressive development of the port – with its crucial trading function – towards the bay.

In the period immediately before the arrival of the Normans, Dublin is estimated to have had a fleet of over 200 trading ships, plying routes to distant continental and Scandinavian ports as well as to major towns in the west of England. Of these, Chester and Bristol were the most important. There was also an important shipbuilding yard in the town.

The next major development in the city's history was the product of an intrigue and a turbulent life. Diarmait Mac Murchada, the king of Leinster whom we have already seen founding a convent in the city, displayed a more secular attitude to women by abducting one Dergovilla, the wife of a minor regional king called O'Rourke. Whether the lady consented to be abducted or not is unclear, but the upshot was that O'Rourke – understandably humiliated to be made a cuckold – appealed to Rory O'Connor, the king of Connacht and the provincial ruler with the nearest claim to call himself high king. O'Connor's muscle saw Mac Murchada lose his kingdom. He was forced to flee abroad.

Diarmait eventually found his way to the Norman king of England, Henry II, then on campaign in Aquitaine. Henry was sympathetic but could not spare any of his troops to help Diarmait recover his kingdom. He did, however, however, give him letters authorising him to raise troops in Henry's lands back in Britain. In return, Diarmait pledged to hold Leinster as Henry's vassal and to offer his daughter's hand to whatever military leader might be found in Henry's lands.

This possibility immediately secured a potential interest for the crown of England in the island of Ireland. There was already the uncertain ecclesiastical loyalty of the see of Dublin to confuse the issue, not to mention a papal bull of 1155, Laudabiliter, which authorised Henry II to invade Ireland in order to enforce religious conformity. This bull was almost certain prompted by the see of Canterbury – nettled by the "transfer" of Dublin to Armagh's jurisdiction under terms of the Synod of Kells. Moreover, Canterbury would have had a ready ear in Pope Adrian IV (Nicholas Breakspear, the only Englishman ever to hold the office). The net effect was that Henry II had a papal warrant to invade Ireland should it suit him. It did not, but he had no objection to helping Diarmait recover his kingdom.

And so it was done. The story has been told a thousand times. Diarmait raised troops in Wales, returned and recovered some of his lands in 1167, was reinforced by more Norman troops that land in 1169 and an even more formidable force in 1170. Its leader was Richard fitzGilbert, deposed Earl of Pembroke, known to history as Strongbow. It was he who claimed the hand of Diarmait's daughter Aoife.

Strongbow and his men captured Dublin in that same year. The Anglo-Norman era had begun.

Jackeen

From its earliest foundation by the Vikings, Dublin has instinctively looked east. Its original purpose was to serve as a link in a chain of Viking trading towns on either side of the Irish Sea. Its early life was wholly orientated eastward, to the sea.

This eastward orientation has been a consistent feature of Dublin's life throughout its history. It has always retained its trading function as the principal centre for the import and export of goods to the island. From Norman times, it became the centre of English royal power, in effect the capital of the country – although that term did not acquire its modern weight of meaning until after the French Revolution.

It was, however, at all times the largest city in Ireland and that, combined with its status as a centre of royal power, marked it out as a place apart. This feature was exaggerated in medieval times when effective royal power was exercised only in the Pale, the narrow area girdling the city to the west. The rest of the island was a series of magnate estates and semi-independent Gaelic kingdoms.

The difference of Dublin was further exaggerated as it expanded towards its Georgian apogee in the eighteenth century. It was by far the largest city in the country, the centre of fashion and wealth, the location of the Irish parliament and the higher courts, the site of the country's only university and other institutions of scholarship and learning like the Royal Dublin Society and the Royal Irish Academy.

Furthermore, it was, until relatively late in historical time, a Protestant city in an overwhelmingly Catholic island. Its proximity to England, as well as its status as a port city, left it disproportionately open to English influence, not least in language. Although Irish was spoken in the city until the nineteenth century, English was the language of the ruling elite and the commercial classes.

Inevitably, the otherness of Dublin was marked in the eyes of rural Ireland. The back country is always suspicious of the city – and especially of a port city with its promiscuous openness to new ideas and fashions. Yorkshire sniffs at London; the Highlands at Edinburgh; Tennessee at New York.

This distance between a relatively anglicised Dublin and a rural hinterland that was progressively less so, especially the farther south and west one went, became important in the nationalist period from 1800 on. Nationalism was the project of an overwhelmingly Catholic and rural populace, a union of interests that deepened after the mid nineteenth-century Great Famine. The church acquired a moral monopoly over the nationalist community and the settlement of the land question became entwined with the nationalist demand.

In effect, the farmers came to see themselves as the true people of Ireland, an illusion from which they have never quite retreated. This compounded normal rural suspicion of the city and it became common to caricature Dublin as an English redoubt, John Bull's beachhead in Ireland. Thus the pejorative term Jackeen to describe a Dubliner, being a version of little Jack [John] Bull. Interestingly, the term was normally applied to "native" working-class Dubliners rather than to the middle classes, many of whom were of recent provincial origin.

And there was some justification for this. Working-class Dublin did adopt some English habits that rural Ireland generally did not. Trades unions – many of them Irish branches of English parents – were one important part of working-class life. It was no accident that nationalism, an overwhelmingly rural and petit bourgeois phenomenon, was generally hostile to the unions, suspecting them of weakening national unity and sowing dissent. Likewise, the Dublin poor took to association football – soccer – the classic British urban working-class sport, in contrast to their middle-class townsmen (rugby) and the people of the countryside (Gaelic games). The sense of difference, first expressed by the Viking gaze eastward, has endured.

Soccer, or Association Football, established itself more strongly in Dublin than in most other parts of Ireland. This photograph shows one of the oldest Dublin clubs, Bohemians, in black and red stripes, in action.

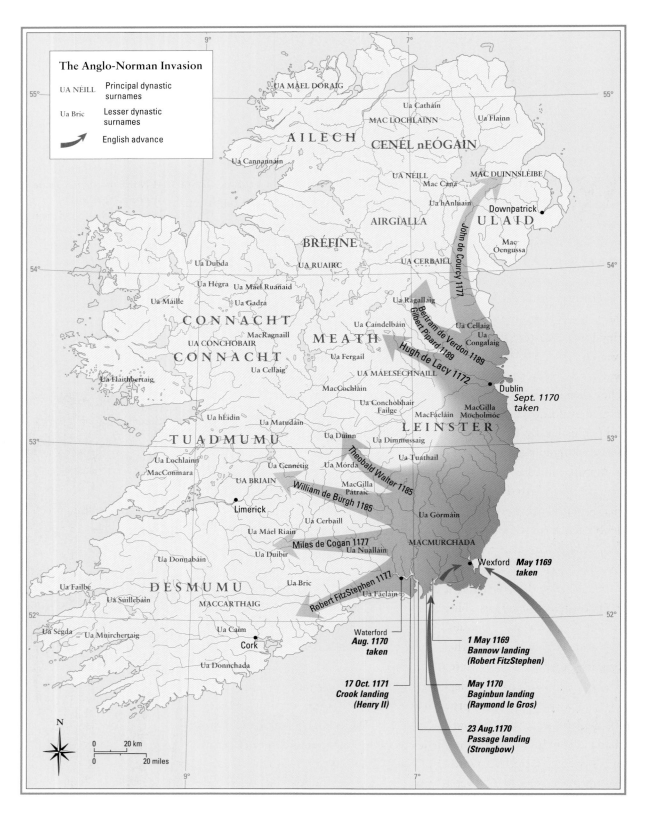

The Anglo-Norman Invasion

UA NÉILL Principal dynastic surnames

Ua Bric Lesser dynastic surnames

English advance

Ua MÁEL DÓRAIG

Ua Catháin

MAC LOCHLAINN

Ua Flainn

AILECH

CENÉL nEÓGAIN

Ua Cannannáin

MAC DUINNSLÉIBE

UA NÉILL

Mac Cana

Downpatrick

AIRGÍALLA

ULAID

Ua hAnluain

Mac Óengussa

BRÉFINE

John de Courcy 1177

UA CERBAILL

Ua Dubda

UA RUAIRC

Ua Ragallaig

Ua Hégra

Ua Máel Ruanaid

Bertram de Verdon 1189

Ua Cellaig

Ua Congalaig

Ua Máille

Ua Gadra

Gilbert Pipard 1189

Ua Caindelbáin

CONNACHT

MacRagnaill

MEATH

Hugh de Lacy 1172

UA CONCHOBAIR

Ua Fergail

CONNACHT

Ua Cellaig

UA MÁELSECHNAILL

Dublin

Ua Flaithbertaig

MacCochláin

Sept. 1170 taken

Ua Conchobair Failge

MacFácláin

MacGilla Mocholmóc

Ua hÉidin

Ua Matudáin

Ua Duinn

LEINSTER

TUADMUMU

Ua Dimmussaig

Ua Lochlainn

Ua Gennétig

Ua Mórda

Ua Tuathail

MacConmara

Theobald Walter 1185

UA BRIAIN

MacGilla Patraic

William de Burgh 1185

Limerick

Ua Cerbaill

Ua Gormáin

Ua Máel Riain

MACMURCHADA

Miles de Cogan 1177

Ua Duibir

Ua Nualláin

Wexford May 1169 taken

Ua Donnabáin

Ua Bric

Robert FitzStephen 1177

Ua Fácláin

Ua Failbe

DESMUMU

Ua Ségda

Ua Muirchertaig

Ua Súillebáin

MACCARTHAIG

Ua Caim

Waterford
Aug. 1170
taken

1 May 1169
Bannow landing
(Robert FitzStephen)

Cork

17 Oct. 1171
Crook landing
(Henry II)

May 1170
Baginbun landing
(Raymond le Gros)

Ua Donnchada

23 Aug.1170
Passage landing
(Strongbow)

N

0   20 km

0   20 miles

— CHAPTER 3 —
NORMANS

Who were these guys? The Normans had originally been a Viking army that established itself in north-west France in the tenth century. Under an agreement of 911 CE known as the Treaty of Saint-Clair-Sur-Epte, the Carolingian King Charles the Simple granted territory around Rouen for settlement by the followers of Rollo, the Viking chieftain. This was the remote origin of the Duchy of Normandy.

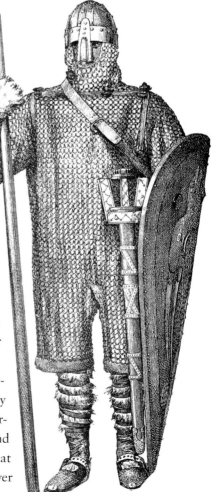

A Norman warrior. These well-equipped and professional fighting men found opportunities to exploit their proficiency well beyond the borders of Normandy.

The presence of a Viking duchy across the channel was a worry for the kings of Anglo-Saxon England, for whom the presence of Viking kingdoms in eastern England was a constant anxiety. Gradually, however, the Vikings of Normandy became thoroughly assimilated in their new land and from about 1000 CE we can speak of them as French. They then emerged as one of the most remarkable expansive forces in medieval Europe. They sent bands of adventurers into the Italian peninsula. By 1130, they had ousted the Saracens and established a kingdom in southern Italy and Sicily, which over time was to mutate into the famous Kingdom of the Two Sicilies. Their own rule only lasted a mere sixty-four years before the kingdom yielded to the rising power of the Hohenstaufen, but they left an indelible mark on the region and were the leading force in the establishment of the Christian kingdom in Palestine in 1099 following the First Crusade.

By the time the Normans' Italo-Sicilian kingdom foundered in 1194, their cousins were long established in England which they had conquered in 1066. The Norman Conquest wrought the destruction of Anglo-Saxon England and transformed the country. Just over a century later, their knights under Strongbow were in Ireland.

They captured Dublin, deposing the last Viking ruler Askulv and resisting his attempt at recapture. They also resisted an attempt by Rory O'Connor, the soi-disant high king, to take the city. Diarmait Mac Murchada died in his hour of triumph, leaving Strongbow as lord of Dublin and much of eastern Ireland. Word of all this reached Henry II who, fearing that Strongbow would do a "reverse Diarmait" and use his Irish base to recover

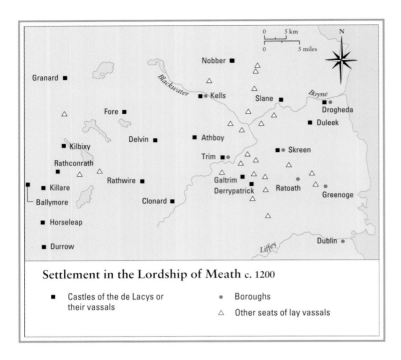

Settlement in the Lordship of Meath c. 1200

- ■ Castles of the de Lacys or their vassals
- ● Boroughs
- △ Other seats of lay vassals

his lost earldom of Pembroke or – worse – set up a separate lordship in Ireland, decided to take a hand. He came to Ireland, made a show of force, and secured the loyalty of Strongbow and Dublin and the submission of many Irish chiefs.

Dublin now ceased to be an independent city state but instead became a dependency of the crown of England. But England in turn was in the power of foreign French-speaking conquisadores. French was the language of law and power and the country's interests were thoroughly aligned with France where King Henry II was Count of Anjou, Duke of Normandy, Duke of Aquitaine, Duke of Gascony and Count of Nantes. He was a great-grandson of William the Conqueror, which accounted for some of his French titles. The others were acquired through his marriage to Eleanor of Aquitaine, the former wife of King Louis VII of France.

All this introduced Dublin to the usages of continental urban government and its representative institutions. The key document in this process was the royal charter. This was a grant of lands and privileges from the crown. The grant was usually made in perpetuity, thus giving legal certainty. Henry granted Dublin to the freemen of Bristol, extending to them privileges similar to those that they enjoyed back home. Of these, the most important were the right to trade free of tolls and customs duties. Others included protection against the financial depredations of sheriffs and municipal self-government with elections for magistrates, burgesses and aldermen. In short, the granting of the charter gave Dublin a legal personality in English medieval law. The royal grant of rights had the same effect as an act of parliament or the decision of an appellate court would have today. It was the authoritative and uncontested source of municipal legitimacy for the Norman town. As such, it emphasised the unique authority of the king as the sole source entitled to grant such a charter of rights.

We may now begin to use the word city rather than town, because while the population and extent of twelfth-century Dublin hardly merits the term, the granting of the charter does. The definition of a city in the Anglo-Norman tradition was a place held by royal charter or enjoying cathedral status. Indeed, the Normans placed even greater emphasis than before on religious foundations.

The number of secular parishes increased as did the number of monastic establishments. These were rich foundations, generously endowed, and they played an important role in charity works as well as in the physical development of city outside the walls. As major landowners, they had a corporate interest in what we would now call property development. They were worldly men, not simply the pious contemplatives of caricature.

Of the ecclesiastical structures outside the walls, the most important was the church of St Patrick which was built by Archbishop John Comyn and dedicated in 1192. Built on the site of a Patrician well on what was then an island in the River Poddle, it was raised to cathedral status in 1213 by Archbishop Henry de Londres following a dispute with Christ Church. Thus there now stood two cathedrals within a kilometre of each other, one inside the walls and one without. They still stand today, although hardly any of the fabric of the original buildings remains – both were the innocent victims of well-intentioned but clumsy Victorian restoration – and the wall between them, of course, has completely disappeared. St Patrick's is the national cathedral of the Church of Ireland, Christ Church the diocesan cathedral of the archdiocese of Dublin.

Not everything happened at once, but Henry II's charter of 1171 was the beginning of a process. Twenty years later, King John issued a further charter. By 1229, municipal self-government had developed to the point that the city had its first elected mayor and council, which met in the Tholsel or town hall. The word derived from the Anglo-Saxon for toll hall, or a centre at which tolls and excise were paid. Dublin's Tholsel stood opposite Christ Church cathedral on a street called Skinner's Row, now Christchurch Place. The original medieval building was replaced in 1676 by a handsome arcaded structure that survived until it was demolished in 1791. By then, the city was in its Georgian pomp and its corporators felt that they had outgrown a building that they regarded as archaic and which was, in truth, in a dangerous state of repair. This suggests that it

Henry II of England.

The Great Seal of Dublin.

was jerry built in the first place, given that it was barely a century old. The corporation worthies then removed to the City Assembly Rooms in South William Street – now the Dublin Civic Museum – before finally taking over the magnificent Royal Exchange in 1852 and reconstituting it as the City Hall. It retains that role today.

Once the Normans were established, there was only one serious attempt made to overturn their settlement. In 1175, Rory O'Connor laid siege to the city and failed. Thereafter the city stood secure. The walls were augmented and strengthened. Dublin Castle was built in the early thirteenth century, standing astride the ridge on the rising ground just south of the river. Although much added to in later centuries, it remained on the same site. The principal medieval survivals in the Castle complex are the Record and Bermingham Towers. It remained the centre and symbol of English royal power in Dublin until 1922.

The charter grant to the men of Bristol emphasised an enduring feature of the city's life. Dublin faced both ways, towards the sea and towards the Irish hinterland to its rear. Of the two, the sea was the more important. The Viking town had formed as a maritime entrepot and manufacturing centre. It retained these essential functions in medieval times, symbolised by the link to Bristol. It also gave the city the air of an English redoubt, with its back turned to the Gaelic hinterland. Many maritime cities have this quality: London itself, New York, Sydney, Istanbul – places whose municipal self-possession leaves them relatively indifferent to the country behind. For much of its history, it makes better sense to see Dublin not as the principal city on the island of Ireland but as a colonial city state like Dubrovnik was to Venice. After the Reformation, Dublin remained a Protestant city in a Catholic island until the nineteenth century. Because we know it as the capital of Ireland does not mean that it was always so, or that its status was not utterly different to that of the present day.

The lifeblood of Norman Dublin was trade and manufacture. That meant the introduction of the guild system to the city. Merchant or trade guilds were associations formed by the practitioners of various avocations for mutual protection and the maintenance of standards. They combined the functions of primitive trade unions and producers' monopolies. Unless a person held membership of the relevant guild, he could not practise the trade concerned. Membership of the early Dublin guilds was confined to "persons of English name and blood", thus further emphasising ethnic exclusivity. This latter prescription was flexibly interpreted, because the Dublin guild merchant roll listed members not just of English provenance but from continental Europe as well. But the bottom line was: no Gaels.

In all, there were twenty-five Dublin guilds, each of which had representa-

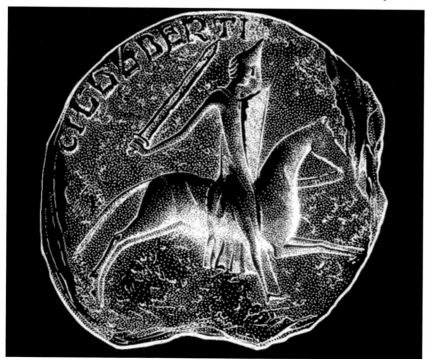

The seal of Strongbow, first Norman Lord of Dublin.

tion on the city corporation. The municipal privileges attaching to guild membership lasted until the passage of the Municipal Corporations Act 1840, which went a long way to democratising urban government. But for six centuries, the trade and merchant guilds were an essential element in the city government.

Early Norman Dublin boomed economically. The population grew rapidly and by the first half of the thirteenth century more than half the inhabitants lived outside the walls. The city pushed west towards Kilmainham, north into Oxmantown and south towards St Patrick's. Some suburban areas without the walls were denominated as Liberties, that is palatinate jurisdictions under the rule of local magnates to whom specific privileges were granted. These included the administration of justice and other functions normally exercised by the municipal authorities. There were a number of such Liberties in the early Dublin suburbs, of which the most prominent were those of St Sepulchre – granted to the Archbishop – and of St Thomas Court and Donore which belonged to the abbey of St Thomas. Indeed, the suburbs themselves tended to cluster around powerful religious foundations.

After the dissolution of the monasteries in 1539, the Liberty of St Thomas Court and Donore was transferred to William Brabazon, whose descendants were to become the Earls of Meath. Thus this area became known in time as the Earl of Meath's Liberties. Today it is simply called the Liberties. Perhaps the vitality of medieval Dublin's growth can be conveyed by one of the principal streets in the Liberties, New Street. It dates from the thirteenth century.

On the riverfront, the gradual process of embanking the river to create a deeper channel for merchant shipping went on apace. Indeed, this was to be a constant in the city's life, for not only did the river need to be contained but the sandbars in the bay remained a menace to shipping for centuries. The river also needed to be crossed, especially to give access to Oxmantown and St Mary's Abbey. The ancient Atha Cliath and the various structures that had superseded it were replaced by a stone bridge, the first in the city's history, in 1215. It remained the only river crossing until the seventeenth century. Stone houses began to appear as well, whereas the Viking town had comprised post and wattle dwellings only. Of course, stone construction was a luxury for the rich. Yet the surviving evidence of domestic stone construction is further evidence of economic growth.

The fourteenth century was a disastrous times in Europe. One distinguished historian has written that "its disorders cannot be traced to any one cause; they were the hoofprints of more than the four horsemen of St John's vision, which had now become seven – plague, war, taxes, brigandage, bad government, insurrection, and schism in the Church".

Dublin did not escape these miseries. In 1315, Edward Bruce, brother of

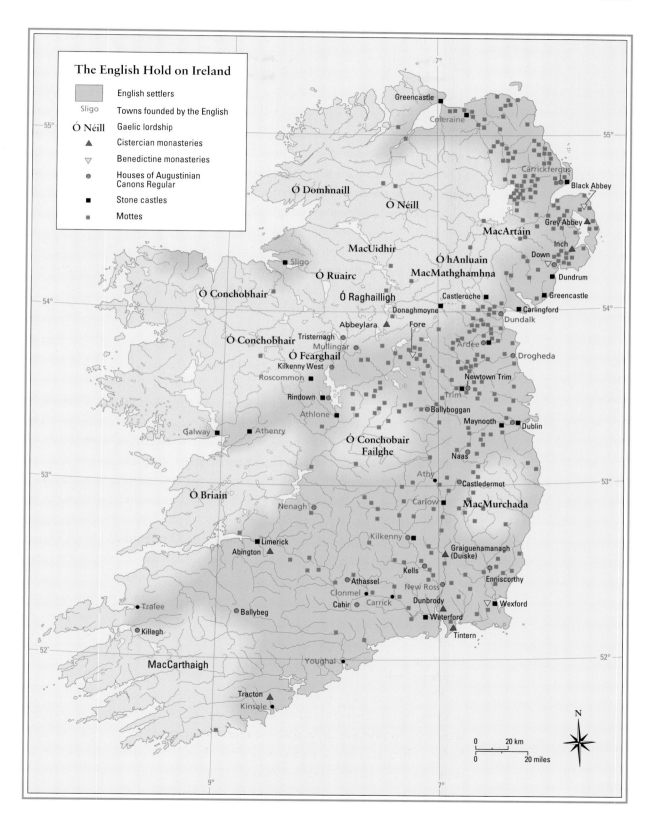

The English Hold on Ireland

- English settlers
- *Sligo* — Towns founded by the English
- Ó Néill — Gaelic lordship
- ▲ Cistercian monasteries
- ▽ Benedictine monasteries
- ● Houses of Augustinian Canons Regular
- ■ Stone castles
- ▪ Mottes

Greencastle

Coleraine

Carrickfergus

Black Abbey

Ó Domhnaill

Ó Néill

MacArtáin

Grey Abbey

MacUidhir

Ó hAnluain

Inch

Down

MacMathghamhna

Sligo

Ó Ruairc

Dundrum

Ó Conchobhair

Ó Raghailligh

Castleroche

Greencastle

Donaghmoyne

Carlingford

Ó Conchobhair

Abbeylara

Fore

Dundalk

Tristernagh

Mullingar

Ardee

Ó Fearghail

Kilkenny West

Drogheda

Roscommon

Newtown Trim

Rindown

Trim

Athlone

Ballyboggan

Maynooth

Galway

Athenry

Ó Conchobair Failghe

Naas

Dublin

Ó Briain

Athy

Castledermot

Nenagh

Carlow

MacMurchada

Limerick

Kilkenny

Abington

Graiguenamanagh (Duiske)

Kells

Enniscorthy

Athassel

New Ross

Clonmel

Dunbrody

Wexford

Tralee

Cahir

Carrick

Ballybeg

Waterford

Killagh

Tintern

MacCarthaigh

Youghal

Tracton

Kinsale

N

0   20 km

0   20 miles

Robert the Bruce, victor of Bannockburn and king of Scotland, led an invasion force to Ireland. Edward was heir presumptive to his brother but he now proceeded to style himself king of Ireland. In this ambition, he had the support of at least some northern Gaelic chiefs. He landed at Larne in May 1315 and began an erratic three-year campaign, which ended with his defeat and death at Faughart, near Dundalk. The details of Bruce's campaign need not concern us here, other than to note that in February 1317 he presented himself in the western approaches to the city – in the region of modern Castleknock – with the clear intention of capturing it.

The response was decisive, ruthless and perhaps a bit panicky. To block his approach, the walls were strengthened and the suburbs burned. This was no small undertaking. The suburbs were more populous than the compact walled centre. They generated more tax revenue for the municipal authority. The retreat of such a number of citizens into the already crowded walled city must have created all the pressures that one can readily imagine in a medieval siege. Sanitation alone would have been a nightmare. The fact that the Bruce campaign in Ireland coincided with a three-year famine across north-west Europe compounded the potential misery. The famine is estimated to have killed one in ten of the population of Europe.

But the great fire did the job in the short run. Bruce hesitated. And as he did, an English force under Mortimer landed at Youghal and began to push towards Dublin. Bruce decided not to besiege the city. Instead he withdrew, to continue what remained of his incoherent campaign. The city had saved itself, but at a terrible price. Much of its physical expansion over the course of the preceding century was destroyed in the great fire. Within a generation, as it struggled to rebuild, an even greater disaster struck.

The Genoese trading port of Caffa (modern Feodosiya) in the Crimea is about as far as one can go from Dublin and still be in Europe. It was here that the deadly plague bacillus first announced itself in Europe in 1347. It had probably been carried along the Silk Road from China and central Asia. It was better known as bubonic plague – because its physical symptoms were the presence of buboes or swellings, generally in the armpits and the groin. Most people who contracted it died within a week, which made it a terrifying presence. It was carried along trade routes by rats which transmitted it to humans. This made port cities especially vulnerable to the pandemic.

From Caffa, it was carried west by fleeing Genoese traders who introduced it to Italy. From there it spread like a bush fire across the continent. It is estimated to have killed about a quarter of the total population of Europe – perhaps as many as 25 million people – although its effects were generally more lethal in the Mediterranean lands than in the north and west. Still, casualty rates in England are estimated at about 20 per cent of the entire population and there is little reason to doubt that the Irish figure was very different.

The populations of Europe were in a poor condition to resist. The same climate changes – colder, wetter winters – which were typical of the early fourteenth century had reduced crop yields and contributed to the famine of 1315–18. This was a classic subsistence crisis arising from a preceding period of economic expansion. Populations had grown in the thirteenth century; now the climate had turned and famine was the consequence. Even when the famine passed, nutrition levels generally were poor in the first half of the century. People's systems were ill equipped to deal with any plague, let alone one as virulent as this.

The Black Death reached Dublin in August 1348. In a malignant example of medieval globalisation, it had taken barely a year to travel the trade routes from one end of Europe to the other. By Christmas that year, it is estimated to have killed 14,000 people in the city.

The Black Death had a devastating effect on populations right across Europe in the 1340s.

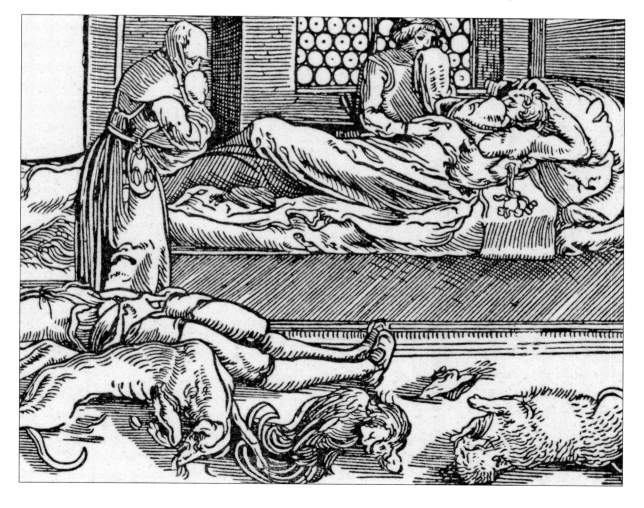

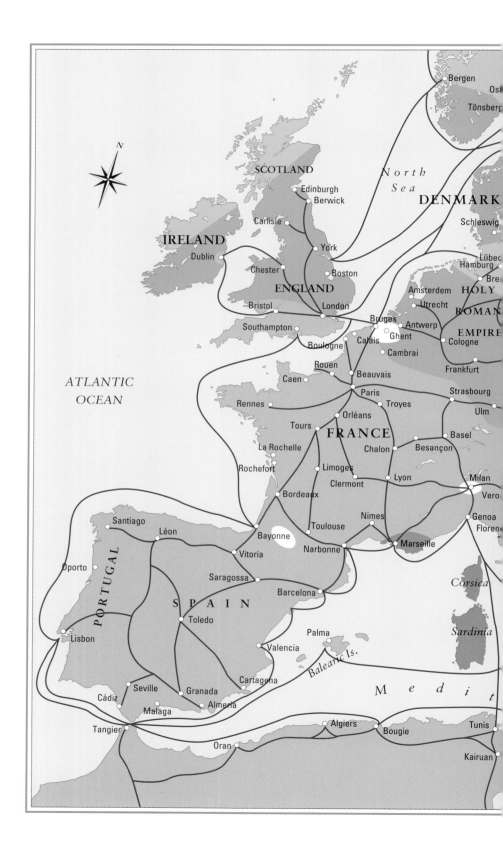

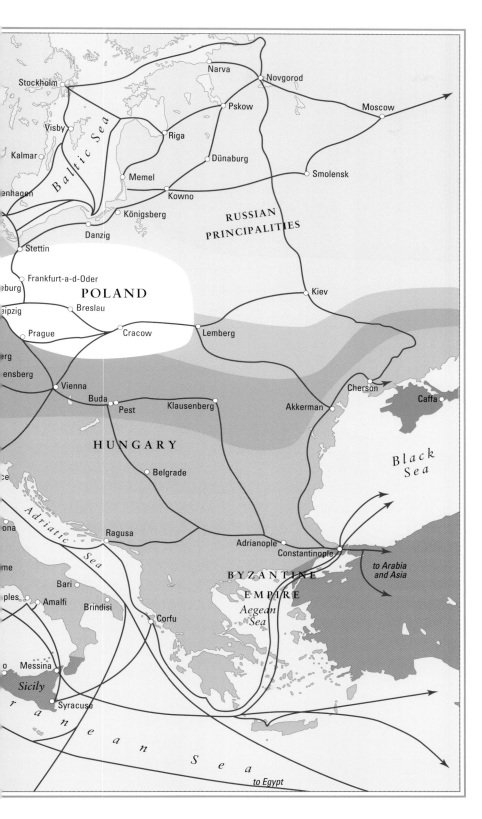

Stockholm

Narva

Novgorod

Pskow

Moscow

Visby

Riga

Kalmar

Dünaburg

Baltic Sea

Memel

Smolensk

enhagen

Kowno

Königsberg

RUSSIAN
PRINCIPALITIES

Danzig

Stettin

Frankfurt-a-d-Oder

eburg

POLAND

Kiev

eipzig

Breslau

Prague

Cracow

Lemberg

erg

Vienna

ensberg

Buda

Cherson

Caffa

Pest

Klausenberg

Akkerman

HUNGARY

Black
Sea

Belgrade

Adriatic

na

Ragusa

Adrianople

me

Constantinople

to Arabia
and Asia

ples

Bari

BYZANTINE

Amalfi

Brindisi

EMPIRE

Corfu

Aegean
Sea

o

Messina

Sicily

Syracuse

r

a

n

e

a

n

S   e   a

to Egypt

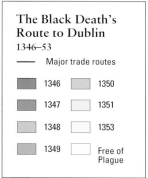

The Black Death's Route to Dublin
1346–53

—— Major trade routes

1346	1350
1347	1351
1348	1353
1349	Free of Plague

Minot

To the south of the city walls lay an ancient well named for and traditionally associated with St Patrick. It stood on marshy ground in an island formed by two branches of the Poddle. The association with the saint proved more persuasive than the unsatisfactory location and a church had stood there since Gaelic times.

In 1192, the archbishop of Dublin, John Comyn, decided to rebuild on this sensitive religious site. He replaced the original church – it may have long since fallen into decay – with a new structure which he named for St Patrick. It was a collegiate church, that is one devoted to scholarship and learning as well as to Christian devotion. Happily, that tradition survives to this day, in the form of St Patrick's grammar school and choir school.

In 1316, that time of misfortune in the city's history, the tower of St Patrick's was blown down in a storm. The archbishop of the day, Thomas Minot, oversaw the rebuilding of the cathedral, including the erection of the new tower – the most prominent feature of the building – that has borne his name ever since. At this time, however, Minot's tower was simply that: a tower. The fleche spire that now rises from it is a much later addition, from 1769.

The church suffered the customary iconoclastic vandalism associated with the Reformation, resulting in the destruction of the medieval statuary. At this time, the 1530s, St Patrick's passed to the reformed Church of Ireland, whose national cathedral it became and remains. Cromwell thought so little of the place that he stabled his horses in the nave – this to show his contempt for Anglicanism, towards which he showed a robust Puritan hostility.

St Patrick's will forever be associated with its most distinguished clergyman, Jonathan Swift, who was dean from 1713 until his death in 1745. The dean is the head of the cathedral. Impressive though this title sounds, it was a sore disappointment to Swift. He had been born in Dublin but looked to make an ecclesiastical and literary career in London, which he did with great success until the ousting of the Tory government, of which he was a staunch supporter, on the death of Queen Anne in 1714. There followed the long Whig hegemony under the first three Georges, by the end of which Swift was long dead. So his return to his native city was a for him an exile and a banishment. Yet from this personal disaster, he fashioned a place in Dublin life and in the history of English literature that is without parallel. He is generally accounted the greatest satirist in the language, and *Gulliver's Travels* alone guarantees his immortality.

Various restoration works were necessitated during the seventeenth and eighteenth centuries, but by the nineteenth it was clear that St Patrick's required a comprehensive restoration appropriate to its status both as the national cathedral of the Established Church and as the largest church building in Ireland. In 1860, Sir Benjamin Lee Guinness, the head of the brewing family, personally underwrote a five-year comprehensive project to completely restore its fabric. He did so with the bull-necked self-confidence typical of many a Victorian tycoon, insisting on a completely free hand independent of any third-party advice, disinterested, expert or otherwise.

The result is the modern cathedral, of which it may be said that we hardly know what's what. The architectural fashion for Gothic revival was sweeping all before it in the 1860s, so the restoration was not dissonant. But it is none the less a vast pastiche. However, better a pastiche, perhaps, than nothing at all: for it can be argued that the brewer saved the church from centuries of neglect punctuated only by emergency repairs.

The plaque marking the burial site of Jonathan Swift in St Patrick's Cathedral.

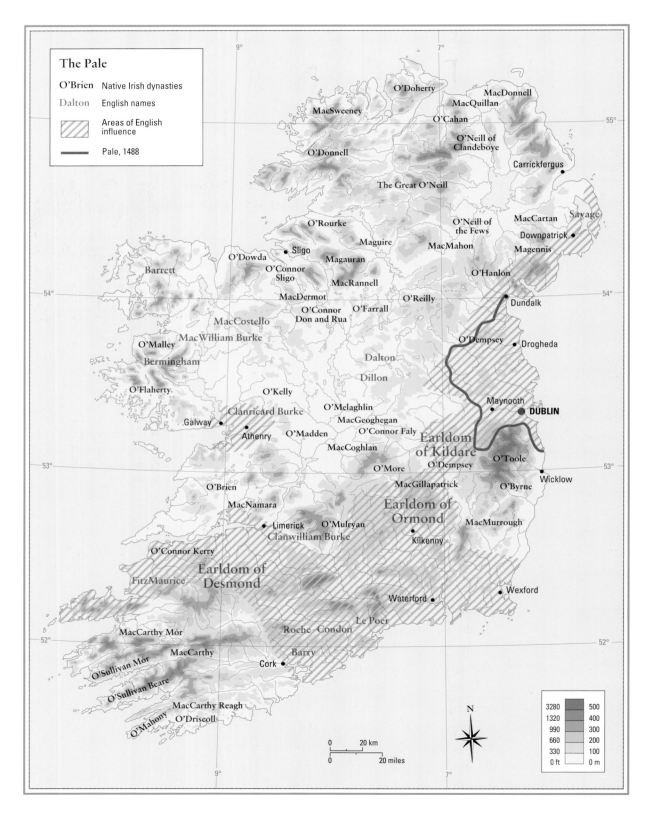

The Pale

O'Brien   Native Irish dynasties

Dalton   English names

Areas of English influence

Pale, 1488

O'Doherty

MacDonnell

MacQuillan

MacSweeney

O'Cahan

O'Neill of Clandeboye

O'Donnell

Carrickfergus

The Great O'Neill

Savage

O'Rourke

O'Neill of the Fews

MacCartan

Downpatrick

Maguire

MacMahon

Magennis

O'Dowda

Sligo

Magauran

O'Hanlon

Barrett

O'Connor Sligo

MacRannell

O'Reilly

Dundalk

MacDermot

O'Connor Don and Rua

O'Farrall

O'Dempsey

Drogheda

MacCostello

Dalton

MacWilliam Burke

Dillon

O'Malley

Bermingham

O'Flaherty

O'Kelly

O'Melaghlin

Maynooth

DUBLIN

Clanricard Burke

MacGeoghegan

Galway

O'Connor Faly

Earldom of Kildare

Athenry

O'Madden

O'Dempsey

O'Toole

MacCoghlan

O'More

Wicklow

O'Brien

MacGillapatrick

O'Byrne

MacNamara

Earldom of Ormond

Limerick

O'Mulryan

Clanwilliam Burke

MacMurrough

Kilkenny

O'Connor Kerry

FitzMaurice

Earldom of Desmond

Wexford

Waterford

MacCarthy Mór

Le Poer

Roche Condon

MacCarthy

Barry

O'Sullivan Mór

Cork

O'Sullivan Beare

MacCarthy Reagh

O'Mahony

O'Driscoll

N

3280		500	
1320		400	
990		300	
660		200	
330		100	
0 ft		0 m	

0   20 km

0   20 miles

CHAPTER 4
THE PALE AND THE NEW ENGLISH

The disasters of the early fourteenth century had a context. The first Irish parliament had met at Castledermot, Co. Kildare in 1264. It was a body comprised exclusively of Hiberno-Norman magnates and its deliberations represented the concerns and anxieties of the colony. Not the least of these anxieties turned on the gradual contraction of the colony. For most of the thirteenth century, it had prospered and grown. But in the last quarter, from about 1275, the tide turned.

The Norman colonisation had involved the securing of land, usually at the expense of the pre-existing Gaelic owners, and its settlement with tenants from England and Wales who brought with them the more advanced agricultural skills of those countries. By this process, the eastern half of the island had become anglicised. But the push westward, while superficially successful, involved fewer and fewer imported tenants. As a result, the more westerly settlements came to rely on Gaelic labour; the interaction between the "two nations" was more complete and intimate than in the earlier period; inter-marriage and the assumption of Gaelic ways, even to the point of adopting the language, became a fixed feature of these marchlands.

Then the whole colonisation process seemed to go into reverse. Gaelicisation took its place. The colonists were, so to speak, going native. Moreover, the natives themselves offered increasing resistance as the thirteenth century wore on. Lands previously yielded up were regained. Inter-marriage and the adoption of Gaelic language and customs diluted the blood of the colony. A whole series of parliamentary statutes tried in vain to arrest this process. In 1297, the first such proscription forbade the wearing of Gaelic dress and a series of similar bans followed in the new century. The most famous of these were the Statutes of Kilkenny (1366) which outlawed inter-marriage and the use of the Gaelic language while insisting on the use of Common Law rather than the Gaelic Brehon Law. They also prescribed the exclusive use of English nomenclature. They even attempted to regulate horsemanship after the English rather than the Irish fashion and once again banned Gaelic forms of dress. This was an eloquent comment on the doomed legislation of 1297 which had clearly been ignored in the meantime, as the Statutes themselves were to be in the future.

Two ladies from the settled region of the Pale are shown here with 'Kerns', traditionally-dressed and equipped, Irish warriors. The illustration was intended to contrast the civilisation of the Pale with the perceived barbarism of the West.

The mere presence of all this legislative anxiety is rich evidence of the process it wished to reverse. The fourteenth century brought a sustained revival and reassertion of Gaelic power, with the result that the colony changed and contracted. By the late fifteenth century, only a small area around Dublin was securely under the direct control of the English crown. This was the famous Pale, an area running from the foothills of the mountains south of the city westward around the towns of Maynooth and Trim before curving back east to rejoin the sea at the fortified town of Dundalk.

The word pale comes from the Latin palus, a stake. It refers to stakes as boundary markers and that is essentially what the Pale was: a fortified defen-

Spread of the Black Death 1348–1350

The Black Death arrives in 1348

Plague spreads from south-east to north and west covering the whole of Ireland by 1350

sive border marking the outer limit of that territory when the king's writ ran. It was elastic, contracting more often than expanding as the fifteenth century wore on. The rough area identified above marks its smallest extent at the end of the century.

Beyond the Pale, one found what were in effect palatinate lands held by Hiberno-Norman magnates such as the earls of Kildare, Ormond and Desmond, or lands still in Gaelic ownership.

For Dublin, this period confirmed its status as a provincial link in the Anglo-Welsh maritime world, ever more cut off from the greater Irish hinterland. It seemed that its glory days were behind it. The triple blow of famine, the great fire and the Black Death had enfeebled the urban fabric. The stone bridge had been dismantled in 1316 in order to reinforce the walls in the face of the Bruce threat. It was rebuilt only to collapse in 1385 and not to be rebuilt again until 1428.

When King Richard II of England came to Ireland twice at the end of the century – in 1394 and 1399 – he found Dublin in a sorry state. The population had continued to decline ever since the passing of the Black Death earlier in the century. From a pre-plague estimate of 35,000, it may even have fallen below 10,000 by 1400. The reason for the king's visit was the pacification of the Gaelic tribes. To this end, he brought an army of 5,000 in 1394, the largest military force seen in medieval Ireland. Various chiefs submitted to him and then returned to their old ways when he had gone. His second expedition was cut short by the need to return to England to deal with the Bolinbroke rebellion. This he failed to do; he lost his crown and his life and Bolinbroke became Henry IV.

Ballyowen Castle as painted by Gabriel Beranger in the 1750s. It is believed that the castle was originally constructed in the mid-1100s and is typical of the fortified houses and castles that provided a kind of unco-ordinated, but nevertheless useful, defence of the Pale.

The English crown had proved less than effective in pacifying the Gaelic tribes and the city remained vulnerable to attack, especially from the ferocious marauders who lived in the Wicklow Mountains just south of the city. The citizens of the city decided that they must shift for themselves and they inflicted a huge defeat of the Wicklow men in 1402, giving no quarter.

The fifteenth century is the great black hole in the history of Dublin. It is not that nothing happened – that is obviously not true – but nothing of significance happened. It was a century of decline. No great public buildings were constructed. There were no developments in city government, nor any expansion of trade and commerce. Dublin hunched rather nervously behind the shelter of the Pale, a stagnant English trading colony. For instance, there were no additions made to the riverfront embankments between 1300 and 1500. The

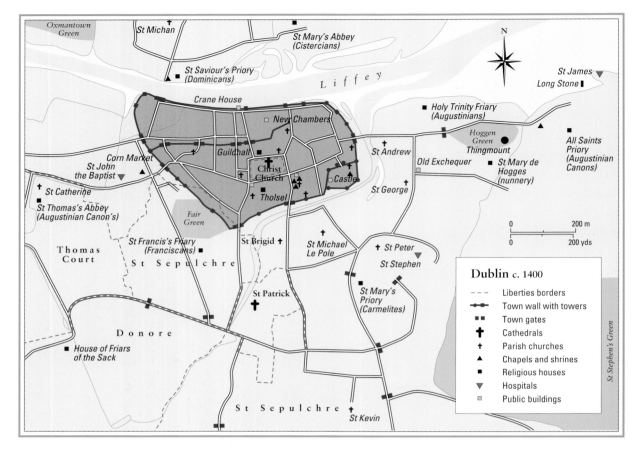

existing system of quays was insufficient to narrow the river channel – essential to deepening it so that it could take bigger ships – and the older defences were in poor repair and not fit for purpose. This compounded the perennial problem of the sandbars in the bay, which made the approaches to the city hazardous for shipping. The result was that larger ships had to use Dalkey Sound for anchorage, with cargoes then being transported into the city by draught animals. Passenger ships usually berthed at Ringsend.

From time to time, the city was drawn into the interminable series of English dynastic struggles known collectively as the Wars of the Roses. The victory of the Lancastrian element at the Battle of Bosworth in 1485 brought the wars to an end, but a Yorkist imposter called Lambert Simnel was crowned King of England in Christ Church cathedral two years later. Simnel then sailed to England to press his claim, was defeated and lived out his life as a kitchen scullion in the royal household.

The Simnel incident reflected the political hazards present in a time of contested kingship. The most powerful Hiberno-Norman magnate family in Ireland, the FitzGeralds earls of Kildare, were Yorkist sympathisers. Yet their domestic power base in Ireland was such that the crown effectively devolved the running of the country to them. For most of the medieval period, the lord-ship Ireland enjoyed a form of devolution under the leadership of a lord deputy sent over by the king. From about 1470 on, the position of lord deputy passed into the hands of the house of Kildare, which held it in more or less unbroken hereditary succession until the 1530s. Yorkist or no, the earls of Kildare were too important to ignore even for a Lancastrian king. This was a normal arrangement in composite royal states until relatively recent historical time. Difficulties of distance and communication and the absence of modern bureaucracies and centralised tax-gathering systems ensured that such practical devolution of power to the regions and the marchlands made sense. In effect, great magnates like the Kildares exercised palatinate powers.

This was the arrangement that was finally challenged and overthrown by the turbulent events of the 1530s. Two forces coalesced to produce what was a revolution from above. First, there was a new theory of kingship abroad in Europe, with a movement towards enhanced royal authority in a centralised royal state. This meant unitary kingdoms and the weakening of regional magnate power. France was the most conspicuous example of this new development. The fullest expression of the process would not be seen until the seventeenth century and the doctrine of the divine right of kings, but the movement towards the centralised royal state was already under way in the early 1500s. Henry VIII wanted to move his kingdom in the same direction. This meant clipping the wings of great magnate palatines such as the Percys in Northumberland and the Kildares in Ireland.

At the same time, he came to assert his independence in ecclesiastical mat-

The 'Record Tower' of Dublin Castle. This medieval survivor remains largely intact within the fabric of the castle as seen today. Dublin Castle remained the adminstrative centre of English power in Ireland until 1922.

This model of Medieval Dublin was constructed for the National Museum of Ireland. Looking from the west towards the east, it shows the city sometime after 1428 when the stone bridge over the River Liffey was re-constructed. The city is over-shadowed by Dublin Castle.

ters. This was more a question of dynastic necessity than of ideology. His queen, Catherine of Aragon, had suffered a series of miscarriages and had only given birth to one daughter, the future Queen Mary, in 1516. He wished to divorce her and marry the younger (and hopefully more fruitful) Anne Boleyn. Henry is often caricatured as an old goat, and he may well have been, but he had good reason to fret over the succession. His father had been the victor of Bosworth back in 1485, so the memory of the chaotic Wars of the Roses was a recent one. The birth of a healthy male heir was essential to the security of the Tudor dynasty.

Normally, a divorce would not have been a problem. The pope understood these dynastic imperatives and would, in the ordinary way of things, have given Henry the necessary dispensation. Unfortunately, in 1527 when the matter came to a head, Pope Clement VII was a prisoner of the Habsburg Emperor Charles V, nephew of Catherine of Aragon. Following the notorious Sack of Rome by imperial troops, the pope was incarcerated in the Castel Sant'Angelo. Charles did not wish to see his aunt humiliated, so he encouraged the pope to dig in his heels with Henry. The consequence was the break with Rome and the establishment of the royal supremacy in the years 1533–36. Thus was born the Church of England, with the Church of Ireland following suit in 1537. Although this was not a theological break – Henry died still believing himself a Catholic – it laid the indispensable foundation for the Reformation in both islands.

The royal supremacy in the church was all of a piece with the drive towards the centralising royal state. In Ireland, the earl of Kildare began to feel the heat. As early as 1519, he had first been summoned to court by Henry to give an account of himself, not being re-appointed lord deputy until 1524. In 1530, he was nominally replaced by Sir William Skeffington but Kildare was still the real power in Ireland. In acknowledgment of this Kildare was reappointed in 1532. In 1534, however – the year that Henry was excommunicated by Rome – Kildare was once more summoned to London. This time he was arrested and clapped in the Tower.

Henry's chief minister, Thomas Cromwell, was already intriguing against the Kildare interest and had allies in the Irish Council in Dublin. Kildare left his son Thomas, Lord Offaly, in charge back home with instructions to be wary of the Irish Council and to ignore any instruction to go to London. Kildare was in poor health when he travelled over as a result of gunshot injuries previously sustained. Offaly, better known to history as Silken Thomas was able to maintain contact with his father. Kildare gave him regular advice, although also informing him that he had been forbidden to return to Ireland. In the meantime, the summons to London duly arrived and with it the belief on Thomas's part that his father had been disempowered by Henry.

What followed was the famous revolt of Silken Thomas. In the words of

Elizabeth Fitzgerald, known popularly as 'The Fair Geraldine' was half-sister to Silken Thomas and Countess of Lincoln.

one historian, "Thomas was not the immature and headstrong fop of legend: the silken epithet was a piece of bardic whimsy". In association with his advisers and the traditional network of Kildare allies, he was attempting to demonstrate that Ireland could not be ruled without the co-operation and support of the traditional Kildare power base. Still, his defiance of the king went beyond anything that the Kildare faction had ever attempted previously. They were soon to discover that Henry was not a man to be defied.

On 11 June 1534, Silken Thomas and a retinue of over 100 horsemen burst in upon a meeting of the Irish Council in St Mary's Abbey, on the north bank of the Liffey. He resigned as vice-deputy, handing over the ceremonial sword of office to the lord chancellor. He then withdrew to Oxmantown, where he had troops billeted. This action was taken on the direct advice of his father and with the support of his advisers in Ireland. When word of this action reached London, Kildare was promptly clapped in the Tower, where he died – whether from the injuries previously sustained or from poison is unknown – in September.

What made the rebellion of Silken Thomas different was the religious issue. Thomas denounced Henry as an apostate and called for allegiance to pope and emperor, to whom he sent emissaries soliciting aid for his cause. He also called for the expulsion of all Englishmen from the lordship of Ireland. This led to the capture of the archbishop of Dublin, John Alen, who was indeed English and who was duly murdered.

This was a direct challenge to the Henrician settlement in both church and state. Henry sent Skeffington to Ireland with a substantial army and with formidable artillery. The result was the total defeat Silken Thomas and the destruction of Kildare power for ever. Their hitherto impregnable castle at Maynooth fell to the royal guns. Silken Thomas and five of his uncles were shipped to London and executed. The Kildare power was broken and their vast land holding forfeit to the crown. It was the end of the Middle Ages.

The effect of all this on Dublin was twofold. First, it raised the status of the city from a trading outpost to a centre of royal government. Henry's determination to transform the way in which Ireland was governed was symbolised in 1541 by the creation of the kingdom of Ireland. No longer a mere lordship, it was henceforth to be a sister kingdom. Dublin was now a royal capital, albeit a rather shabby one. More immediately dramatic in its effect on the city's fabric was the dissolution of the monasteries.

The city was rich in religious foundations. As we noted earlier, suburban development tended to cluster around religious houses, which were frequently impressive structures within walled enclosures. It is estimated that 20 per cent of all land in the city, its suburbs and the surrounding county was owned by religious houses. The disappearance of such a large body of long established in-

Nothing survives of the original buildings in Trinity. The oldest surviving buildings in the modern university are the Rubrics between Library Square and New Square which date from 1701.

stitutions had a dramatic effect. All but one of the Dublin monasteries that were suppressed were located in the suburbs, outside the city walls. The most significant of these in later history was the Augustinian Priory of All Hallows, which stood in the far eastern suburbs on a site just south of the river as it opened towards the bay.

All Hallows was suppressed in 1538, the canons were pensioned off and the site was granted to Dublin Corporation in thanks and compensation for the physical damage the city had sustained during the Silken Thomas rebellion. The rebels had made an attempt on the Castle, whose defences were reinforced by stripping bridges and buildings of stone. This was a re-run of the tactic used in the Edward Bruce invasion.

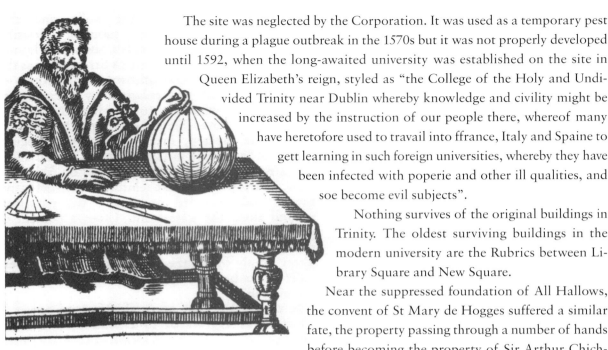

The site was neglected by the Corporation. It was used as a temporary pest house during a plague outbreak in the 1570s but it was not properly developed until 1592, when the long-awaited university was established on the site in Queen Elizabeth's reign, styled as "the College of the Holy and Undivided Trinity near Dublin whereby knowledge and civility might be increased by the instruction of our people there, whereof many have heretofore used to travail into ffrance, Italy and Spaine to gett learning in such foreign universities, whereby they have been infected with poperie and other ill qualities, and soe become evil subjects".

This cartouche from John Speed's Theatre *shows the great man at work.*

Nothing survives of the original buildings in Trinity. The oldest surviving buildings in the modern university are the Rubrics between Library Square and New Square.

Near the suppressed foundation of All Hallows, the convent of St Mary de Hogges suffered a similar fate, the property passing through a number of hands before becoming the property of Sir Arthur Chichester, the lord deputy in 1604. Chichester House was used as the home of the Irish parliament on and off during the seventeenth century before falling into state of disrepair and being demolished in 1728. The foundation stone of the replacement Parliament House was laid in the following year and the magnificent new building – known to us as the Bank of Ireland, College Green – was opened in 1733.

Many other religious houses suppressed in the late 1530s survive vestigially in the city's street names. Thomas Street, Francis Street, John's Lane, Andrew Street, Peter Street, Nicholas Street all take their names from the patron saints of dissolved religious houses. Mary Street recalls St Mary's Abbey, the oldest and richest foundation on the north side. Dame Street, built to connect the Castle to Trinity, takes its name from the church of St Mary del Dam which stood just inside the city walls between where Sycamore Street and Crane Lane now stand. The Dam in question may be a reference to a mill pond or well nearby – there were a number of these on the lower reaches of the Poddle – but equally it may be a simple import of the French word for woman or lady, as in Notre Dame. At the time the church of St Mary del Dam(e) was built, in 1385, the ecclesiastical elite of Dublin would still have been French speaking.

The long reign of Elizabeth I (1558–1603) saw the secure establishment of Protestantism in Britain but not in Ireland. The Irish elite remained Catholic, both Old English (as we shall refer to the Hiberno-Normans from here on) and Gaelic chiefs alike. The allegiance of the elites was key, for in an age of deference it determined the allegiance of the common people. The shared recusancy of the "two na-tions" gave them a common cause, although it required many more generations before the old ethnic suspicions between Gael and Old English were to disappear. Some have even argued that they retain a subterranean existence to the present day.

The term Old English is used to distinguish long-established families of Norman origin from the New English, a very different breed. The New English were the administrators, planters, soldiers and adventurers who came to Ire-land in the years following the Henrician reforms. They were Protestants to a man. The whole history of Ireland in the sixteenth century is the crown's at-tempt to make its writ run throughout Ireland and to reverse the Gaelic revival of the late medieval period that had seen the Pale shrink so badly. This was an enterprise that brought limited success, with plantations in Munster and the midlands following the defeat and dispossession of Old English magnates and Gaelic chiefs alike. The culmination of this process was the Nine Years' war

*John Speed's map,
completed around 1610,
shows a city that has
changed very little over the
preceeding two centuries.*

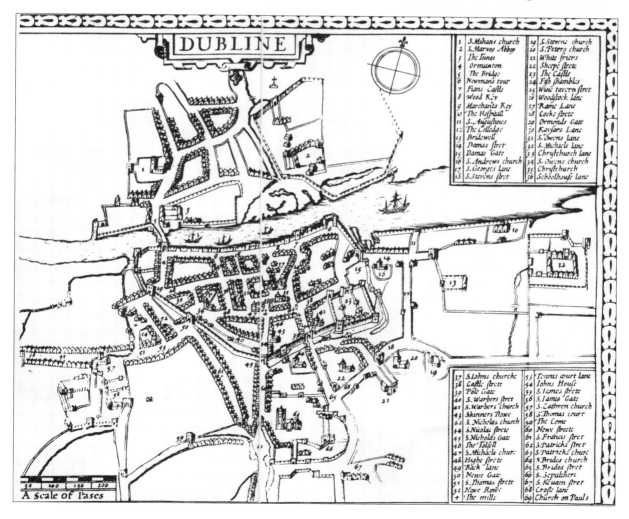

which brought an end to the hitherto impregnable and undefeated world of the Ulster Gaelic lords.

Elizabeth was succeeded in 1603 by James I, whose Irish administration was firmly in the hands of aggressive New English like Chichester and Sir John Davies, the attorney-general. From Dublin Castle, they issued proclamations against religious tolerance – calling for public conformity to the Church of Ireland and attendance at Divine Service – and so harried the defeated Gaelic lords of Ulster that they fled abroad: the famous Flight of the Earls.

The first map of the city of Dublin appeared in 1610. Speed's Map, so called for its maker, is an iconic document. It shows what is still in essence the medieval city. The two and a half centuries since the Black Death had seen no sustained recovery either in commerce or population. Plagues still ravaged the city from time to time. Compared to the vitality and optimism of the thirteenth century, it seemed a paltry legacy. The population was probably no more than 15,000 persons (and Speed's map could be interpreted to yield a lower figure), a poor comparison with the estimate for the early fourteenth century (35,000) and perhaps no more – or little more at best – than the figure for 1400.

The turbulent politics of the 1640s were crucial in the making of modern Ireland. The rebellion of 1641 was principally an attempt to reverse the Plantation of Ulster, which had seen Anglo-Scots settlers take over the lands of the Gaelic earls who had fled. The conspirators plotted to capture Dublin Castle, were betrayed by careless talk and found themselves not in possession of it but incarcerated in it. The 1640s saw Gaelic lords and the Old English make common cause in the Catholic interest. But that interest was ultimately dependent on the good will of the English crown, which under King Charles I was inclined towards religious tolerance – or at least what passed for it in an age of violent religious controversy. Charles lost the English civil war to his parliamentary opponents, who promptly executed him. They were robustly Protestant and it was their military commander, Oliver Cromwell, who landed at Ringsend on 15 August 1649, bent on revenge for Catholic atrocities committed during the failed 1641 rebellion.

By the time he left Ireland less than a year later, he was well on the way to doing what no English ruler since 1170 had managed: the effective subjugation of the entire island and the projection of English law and power into every corner of the land. His regime in England barely survived his death in 1658. Two years later, Charles II, son of the executed king, arrived home from exile in France and resumed the throne as King of England, Scotland and Ireland. To Ireland, he sent as viceroy or lord lieutenant his father's old associate, James, Duke of Ormond, successor to the great medieval Butler dynasty. The duke arrived in Dublin on 27 July 1662, on which date the history of the modern city may be said to begin.

Queen Elizabeth I.

Poynings

For most of the fifteenth century and up until the Tudor revolution in the 1530s, the rule of the English crown in Ireland was devolved to Hiberno-Norman magnate families, of which the FitzGeralds, earls of Kildare, were the most prominent. The power that they held was most completely expressed within the Pale. Outside it, their influence depended as much upon treaty and marriage alliances with Hiberno-Norman and Gaelic families alike as upon main force.

In general this arrangement worked well, or at least in a manner acceptable to London. However, there were inevitable suspicions of magnate rule. In the fluid circumstances of medieval Europe, there was no guarantee that regions owing nominal allegiance to a distant monarch might not form themselves into independent kingdoms. There was no natural law that condemned Bavaria or Catalonia or the great medieval duchy of Burgundy to permanent provincial status. Any one of them could have formed a powerful independent state had historical accident been other than it was.

So too with Ireland. In 1487 the Irish parliament, egged on by the earl of Kildare, declared Lambert Simnel to be Edward, earl of Warwick, son of King Edward IV and therefore the legitimate king of England. The real Warwick was dead, murdered in the Tower of London four years earlier along with his brother by the usurper Richard III, who in turn had been defeated by Henry VII at Bosworth in 1485. Not only did the Irish parliament endorse this Yorkist pretender, Kildare saw him "crowned" in Christ Church cathedral and then raised an army which crossed the Irish Sea and invaded England, being stopped only at the Battle of Stoke.

In the meantime, Kildare ruled in the name of King Edward and even had the Dublin mint strike coins bearing his effigy. Despite this astonishing act of treachery, Henry VII left Kildare in situ for the moment, in itself a fair testimony to his standing. But in 1494, following the appearance of a second Yorkist pretender, Perkin Warbeck – he represented himself to be the other murdered prince in the Tower, Richard duke of York – the king acted decisively. He sent a strong army to Ireland and appointed Sir Edward Poynings as lord deputy. At a parliament in Drogheda, Poynings passed the law that ever after bore his name. It stated that no Irish parliament could henceforth sit without the king's consent, nor any bills be introduced without the prior approval of the king and his council.

The intention was to avoid a repetition of the Simnel fiasco, but the law remained in place until 1782 and became a key bone of contention between the Irish parliament and the crown in the eighteenth century. In fact, it was an unexceptional measure by the standards of its time. Every royal government in Europe tried to circumscribe regional assemblies, lest they become over-mighty.

It was at once a mark of strength and weakness. The crown and the parliament had effective jurisdictional powers only within the Pale. Dublin, at the heart of the Pale, was really a kind of autonomous city state. Here the king's writ ran but only as mediated through his deputy – soon to be Kildare again – and parliament. The city had no formal political relationship with the rest of the island, only such allegiances as were secured by trading, commerce and marriage alliances. By the same token its connection to the crown, while nominally strong, was tempered by the devolved nature of medieval government. There were many contemporary analogues for the relationship between Dublin and London: Venice and Dubrovnik; Constantinople and Salonika; Paris and Toulouse.

Malahide Castle, one of the few surviving great houses of the Pale.

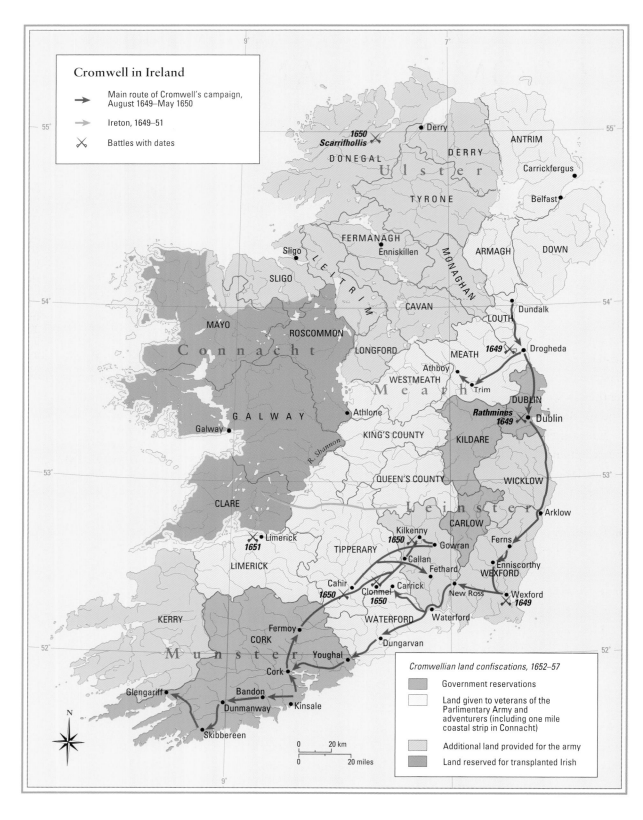

Cromwell in Ireland

→ Main route of Cromwell's campaign,
August 1649–May 1650

→ Ireton, 1649–51

✕ Battles with dates

Cromwellian land confiscations, 1652–57

▨ Government reservations

☐ Land given to veterans of the
Parlimentary Army and
adventurers (including one mile
coastal strip in Connacht)

▨ Additional land provided for the army

▨ Land reserved for transplanted Irish

CHAPTER 5
CROMWELL AND
THE DUKE

The country that the Duke of Ormond inherited had been transformed by Oliver Cromwell who, in the famous phrase, had "like a lightning passed through the land". His direct effect on Dublin was minimal. He stabled his horses in St Patrick's cathedral, but apart from inflicting that indignity he left no lasting physical imprint on the city.

However, he changed the entire context of the city's life. By dispossessing the vast majority of Catholic landowners in the provinces of Leinster and Munster and settling the lands on New English landlords, he put in place a colonial ruling class. Land ownership meant political and economic power in the pre-industrial age. The dispossession of the old elite – Old English and Gaelic alike, Catholics to a man, and all of them come of families established in Ireland for centuries – to be replaced by a new Protestant gentry was meant to secure Ireland for the English interest and for the Reformation. It was a revolution.

It meant that three of the four Irish provinces – the poorest, Connacht, being the exception – were now firmly in New English and Protestant hands. Cromwell had made no distinctions on ethnic grounds. To him, Old English and Gaels were all Catholics and were equally complicit in the outrages committed in the 1641 rebellion. This is an important moment in Irish history, when the sheer pressure of a revolution from above creates a new consciousness, substituting religious solidarity for ethnic identity as the key variable. After Cromwell, a sense of shared Catholic solidarity and grievance replaces the older distinction between the "two nations" of medieval Ireland. Besides, both had a different kind of "new nation" to live with, in the shape of the parvenu landlords.

The Duke of Ormond faced a delicate task. The Restoration of the monarchy had raised hopes among the dispossessed that the Cromwellian land settlement would be overturned or at least gravely weakened. It soon became clear that neither Ormond nor the king felt willing or able to satisfy these hopes. The new regime was neither strong enough nor secure enough to satisfy such demands. The pattern of land ownership established by Cromwell was to endure until the Land Acts of the late nineteenth and early twentieth centuries broke up the estates and established the former tenants as proprietors.

Ormond's Dublin was beginning to acquire some of the sinews of the mod-

Oliver Cromwell, commander of the Puritan New Model Army, religious zealot, one of England's national heroes and the most reviled name in Irsih history.

ern city. From the early seventeenth century, it had become the sole seat of the Irish parliament. The medieval parliament had been peripatetic, meeting as often in Drogheda or Kilkenny as in Dublin. The century also brought the gradual return of economic growth. Dublin began to expand again, with notable suburban development on the north bank of the Liffey and to the west of the walled city towards Kilmainham. A city that had only ever had one bridge (and, as we saw, not even that for a time in the late Middle Ages) acquired four more between 1670 and 1683. Three of these bridges still exist, although all have been reconstructed over time.

The finest of these new bridges was on the site of the modern Capel Street bridge and represented a further shift of the city's centre of gravity eastward towards the bay. It created a new north-south axis from the Castle and made the development of the northern suburbs beyond a tempting prospect. This is exactly what happened in the great eighteenth-century building boom, with the earliest fashionable Georgian developments located north of the river.

Perhaps the most enduring legacy bequeathed the city by the Duke of Ormond is the Phoenix Park. On his arrival in 1662, he took up residence in the Phoenix Manor which stood on the site of the modern Magazine Fort. He acquired 2,000 acres around the Manor as a viceregal deer park. One of the previous owners from whom he bought the land was Sir Maurice Eustace, the speaker of the Irish House of Commons, whose name lives on in a street in Temple Bar. The duke stocked the park with deer, whose descendants are still to be seen there today.

Another notable Ormond legacy is St Stephen's Green. This had existed from medieval times as a pasture area for cattle and horses in the distant southeast reaches of the small town. By 1664, when its twenty-seven acres were denominated by the Dublin Corporation as a public leisure area it was still distant from the city centre. Building lots were sold to enclose the green and were gradually developed for town houses. There was a problem, however. The route linking Trinity College and the Green was deemed to be "so foule and out of repair that persons cannot pass to the said Green for the benefit of the walks therein". Something had to be done and in 1671 the Corporation set about the improvements that in time led to the development of Grafton Street.

Grafton Street in its modern form dates from 1708 and was named for Charles Fitzroy, 2nd Duke of Grafton, who was the lord lieutenant at the time. He was a grandson of King Charles II: his father, Henry Fitzroy, was (as the surname suggests) the illegitimate son of the king and Barbara Villiers, Duchess of Cleveland, the most beautiful and notorious of the king's many mistresses.

The 1680s brought a building boom to Dublin. Churches were built or rebuilt.

Opposite: *James, Duke of Ormond.*

Francis Place's panoramic drawing of the city in 1698 shows seventeen church towers and spires, giving the cityscape a vertical definition that it had previously lacked. The Liberties became increasingly populated and densely housed. This area also became the centre of Huguenot life in the city. The Huguenots were French Protestants, a community of religious dissenters whose position in France deteriorated throughout the seventeenth century. The French wars of religion in the previous century had been a national disaster and Louis XIV was determined to enforce religious uniformity in the country. This made life increasingly difficult for non-Catholics and so, from the 1660s on, there was a steady stream of Huguenot emigrants to Protestant cities like London and Dublin.

Like many talented exiles, they contributed to their host societies in a manner out of all proportion to their numbers. They were skilled craftsmen, especially talented at textile weaving and silk production. Their industry encouraged the development of these trades in Dublin; the name Weaver Street in the modern Liberties in a reminder of their presence. Huguenot numbers grew hugely after the Revocation of the Edict of Nantes in 1685. This edict, which had been in place in France since 1598, had allowed for a degree of religious tolerance but it was offensive to Louis XIV's desire for religious uniformity. Louis' policies were to find an ironic echo in Ireland in the eighteenth-century penal laws, enacted for a similar purpose in a Protestant milieu.

Most of the 1680s was consumed in the construction of the greatest civic building in seventeenth-century Dublin, and the first one in the city that was unambiguously post-Renaissance in design. The Royal Hospital at Kilmainham was built as a residence for homeless ex-soldiers. The model – intellectual if not architectural – was Les Invalides in Paris. The Royal Hospital was completed in 1687, making it older by a few years than Chelsea Hospital in London. The architect of this splendid building was William Robinson, the surveyor-general of Ireland. (He was also the designer of Marsh's Library, beside St Patrick's cathedral.) It occupies an elevated site well to the west of the seventeenth-century city, standing to the south of the river looking north across to the Phoenix Park on the other bank.

The arcaded inner quadrangle has a distinctly Italian feel to it and its cool classicism is in sharp contrast to the Baroque exuberance of the chapel. It fulfilled its original function until 1927. Following two generations of neglect, it was restored and now houses the Irish Museum of Modern Art.

Institutional developments indicated the city's growth, which was most evident in the increased population, which stood at 50,000 by 1700. The first College of Physicians dates from 1667. Custom Houses were built and renewed, first in 1637 and again thirty years later, marking the growth in the city's seaborne commerce. After the building of Capel Street bridge, it became nec-

essary to move the Custom House to the east of it and the building of 1707 occupied the site of the modern Clarence Hotel before itself being replaced by the present building, Gandon's masterpiece of 1791. The 1707 Custom House was also the first to be built outside the city walls, a significant moment in itself, indicating a growing confidence in the political and military stability of the city. Once again, the growth of Dublin's trade was marked by physical expansion eastward towards the bay.

The upheaval in England known as the Glorious Revolution – it was actually a coup d'etat – saw Charles II's Catholic brother, James II, dethroned in favour of his Protestant nephew, William of Orange, in order to protect the Protestant nature of the state and obviate a Catholic dynasty. While this period saw much upheaval in Ireland – James II's three years on the throne had revived hopes of undoing the Cromwellian settlement – little of it affected Dublin. The completeness of the Williamite victory at the Boyne and Aughrim – the latter the effective end of Old English Catholic resistance to the new order – was a reassurance to the Protestant city.

The opening of the new north-south axis across Capel Street bridge, noted earlier, led to the development of Capel Street in the last quarter of the seventeenth century. It was named for Arthur Capel, Earl of Essex, lord lieutenant from 1672 to 1677. Developed by Sir Humphrey Jervis (a parallel street recalls his name), later lord mayor of the city, it quickly established itself as a centre of fashion and the beau monde. Moreover, it led to the area of Henrietta Street where

St Stephen's Green was first laid out in the early eighteenth century but came into its full glory in the late nineteenth century. This image, from the Lawrence Collection, shows St Stephen's Green north in the 1890s. The pedimented building in the middle background is the Royal College of Surgeons in Ireland.

the first great Georgian developments were to take place in the 1720s and con-firmed the north side – for the moment at least – as the fashionable end of town.

As the seventeenth century turned into the eighteenth and Dublin stood at the beginning of its heroic period, it could reflect with some satisfaction on the preceding half century. Cromwell had, albeit with exemplary brutality, ended the state of flux that had existed in Ireland since the Silken Thomas rebellion over a century before. The Restoration and the brief reign of James II had not disturbed the basic settlement reached in the 1650s. The trade and commerce of the city had revived, especially following the arrival of Ormond and the stabil-ising of normal administration and government. Public spaces were opened up, new bridges spanned the river, Protestant immigrants from France brought new skills and energies to the city's economy, growing wealth was visible in the early development of new city quarters and the Royal Hospital was a symbol in stone of the arrival of the continental Renaissance to Ireland.

It all represented a startling and welcome contrast to the uncertainty and stasis that had plagued the city for 300 years since the Black Death. In reality, that is how long the recovery took, as Dublin moved from trading port to royal stronghold to national capital. For that was what it became in the eighteenth

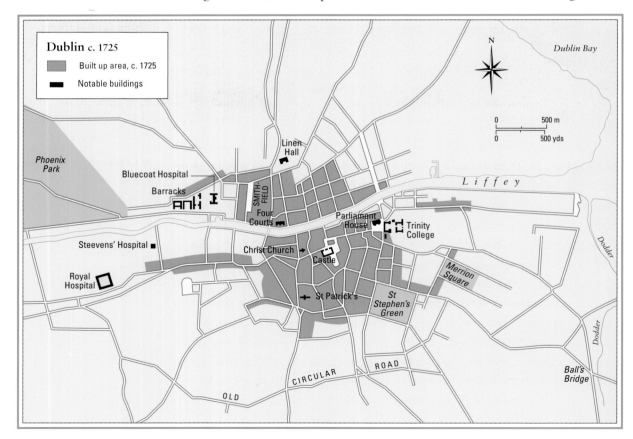

In 1684 the Royal Hospital at Kilmainham was opened, the first major new building in the expansion of Dublin.

century, as the descendants of the Cromwellian settlers grew ever more assured in their victory. Their assurance expressed itself increasingly in a noisy campaign for colonial home rule, asserting the constitutional independence of the kingdom of Ireland from its bigger sister (an assertion that the bigger sister scorned for as long as she could).

It was this class, bound by ties of blood, ethnicity and religion, that dominated the fortunes of eighteenth-century Ireland, in the process raising the capital to European status alike in population, wealth and beauty. They were an all-powerful minority, English by origin, Anglican in religion in a country in which 90 per cent of the population remained Roman Catholic, and alone constituting the political nation. It was not until the 1790s, when their hegemony was about to be fatally challenged, that they acquired the sobriquet by which they are remembered in history. But it is hardly anachronistic to apply it retrospectively. The eighteenth century was the age of the Ascendancy.

Rathmines

By 1649, the confused series of events that had consumed the decade in the three kingdoms of England, Scotland and Ireland had almost resolved themselves. The English civil war between Charles I and parliament had resulted in victory for the latter and execution for the former. In Ireland, most of the country had remained loyal to the king but now prepared to face the wrath of the English parliamentary army under its formidable leader, Oliver Cromwell.

Most of Ireland outside Ulster was under varying degrees of control exercised by James Butler, earl of Ormond, scion of one the oldest and greatest Hiberno-Norman magnate families. His fissiparous coalition was held together only with constant difficulty. At different times, it had the potential to take the whole island in support of the king but Ormond could never realise that potential. In 1647, despairing of the king's cause in Ireland, Ormond surrendered Dublin to representatives of the English parliament.

Thus Dublin resumed its role as a beachhead for the influence of English power – now exercised by the victorious forces of parliament rather than those of the crown – while the rest of the island remained in varying degrees of ambiguous allegiance. It was the Pale by other means. The new parliamentary governor of the city was Colonel Michael Jones, a competent and ruthless officer. He won the battle of Dungan's Hill in Co. Meath against a royalist army and did not scruple to slaughter prisoners to whom quarter had previously been granted.

In 1649, after many vicissitudes and prevarications, Ormond moved his army towards the parliamentary redoubt in Dublin, which he had so lightly surrendered two years previously. His army, in which there were chronic problems of discipline and morale, was not big enough to invest the entire city and it lacked artillery and other siege equipment. Ormond's intention was to starve Jones' garrison by corralling them inside the walls, although how he intended to prevent their being re-supplied and reinforced by sea is not clear.

In the meantime, Oliver Cromwell was marshalling an army at Milford Haven in Wales, bound for Ireland. Perhaps supposing that Cromwell intended to land in Munster – the more probable destination from Milford Haven – Ormond made the fatal error of splitting his forces, some of which he despatched south. In the meantime, Jones had been reinforced by sea and Cromwell was preparing to make for Dublin. His immediate object was to join issue with Ormond's army.

Although the odds against him were lengthening all the time, Ormond pushed on towards the city from the south, reaching as far as Rathmines. He sent a foraging party of about 1,000 men forward to Baggotrath Castle, roughly in the area of the modern Pembroke Road. It took this party, led by a competent officer, the whole night to cover the short distance involved: whether this was due to muddle or treachery on the part of scouts is unknown. At any rate, when they invested Baggotrath, they were hungry and exhausted.

Moreover, Jones was waiting for them. He launched his entire defensive force at Baggotrath, scattering the royalists who fled back whence they had come. The chase continued all the way to Ormond's camp in Rathmines. There, the parliamentarians routed Ormond's forces and finished his army as a fighting force once and for all.

It was the last full-scale battle fought in the environs of the city prior to 1916. Jones' victory meant that Cromwell arrived two weeks later to a country in which there was no longer an organised army capable of offering him resistance.

Colonel Michael Jones, Cromwell's military precursor in Ireland, who ensured that Dublin was secured for the Lord Protector.

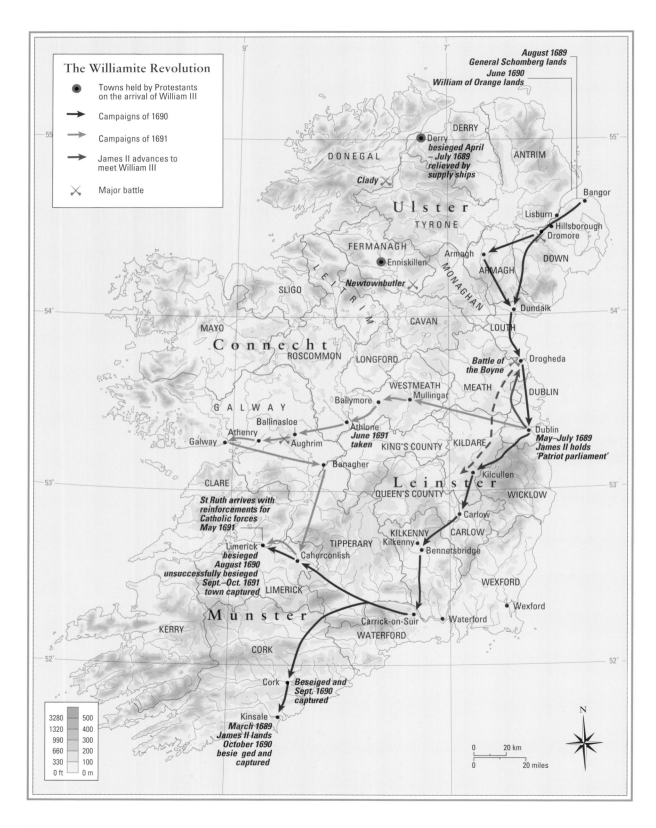

The Williamite Revolution

- ⊙ Towns held by Protestants on the arrival of William III
- → Campaigns of 1690
- → Campaigns of 1691
- → James II advances to meet William III
- ✕ Major battle

August 1689
General Schomberg lands

June 1690
William of Orange lands

DERRY

Derry
*besieged April
– July 1689
relieved by
supply ships*

DONEGAL

ANTRIM

Clady

Bangor

Lisburn

Hillsborough
Dromore

U l s t e r

TYRONE

FERMANAGH

● Enniskillen

Armagh

ARMAGH

DOWN

Newtownbutler ✕

MONAGHAN

Dundalk

SLIGO

LEITRIM

CAVAN

LOUTH

MAYO

C o n n e c h t

ROSCOMMON

LONGFORD

WESTMEATH

MEATH

Mullingar

*Battle of
the Boyne* ✕

Drogheda

DUBLIN

GALWAY

Ballymore

Ballinasloe

Athenry

Galway

Athlone
*June 1691
taken*

KING'S COUNTY

KILDARE

Dublin
*May–July 1689
James II holds
'Patriot parliament'*

Aughrim

Banagher

CLARE

L e i n s t e r

QUEEN'S COUNTY

Kilcullen

WICKLOW

*St Ruth arrives with
reinforcements for
Catholic forces
May 1691*

Limerick
*besieged
August 1690
unsuccessfully besieged
Sept.–Oct. 1691
town captured*

Caherconlish

TIPPERARY

Carlow

CARLOW

KILKENNY

Kilkenny

Bennetsbridge

LIMERICK

WEXFORD

WATERFORD

M u n s t e r

Carrick-on-Suir

Waterford

Wexford

KERRY

CORK

Cork
*Beseiged and
Sept. 1690
captured*

Kinsale
*March 1689
James II lands
October 1690
besie ged and
captured*

3280	500
1320	400
990	300
660	200
330	100
0 ft	0 m

0   20 km

0   20 miles

N

CHAPTER 6
ASCENDANCY

First and always, Dublin has been about the sea. It started as a trading port and the imperatives of seaborne commerce has been central to its history. The year 1707 is, therefore, an important milestone in the story of the city. In that year, parliament passed "An Act for Cleansing the Port, Harbour, and River of Dublin and for Erecting a Ballast Office in the said city". The Ballast Office was the first municipal authority to take control of the port – it had been a prerogative of the crown until this moment – and it quickly made its presence felt.

The key functions of the Ballast Office were the imposition of port charges and the maintenance of the navigation channel, the latter a perennial problem. It also continued the progressive embanking of the river that had begun in earnest in the last quarter of the old century. The construction of the quays on the north bank of the river, collectively to be known as the North Wall, was completed in less than twenty years. Charles Brooking's map of 1728 clearly shows a continuous embanking wall running from around the site of the modern Custom House to a point opposite Ringsend, roughly where the O2 arena stands today. The East Wall was an extension of the North Wall following the line of the present East Wall Road around to Ballybough.

The North and East Walls required constant renewal and maintenance and were greatly improved in the nineteenth century when civil engineering skills were much advanced. But the construction of the originals in such an impressively short time was evidence of the energy which the early Ballast Office brought to the discharge of its duties. The leading traders and merchants of the city – they included such names as Humphrey Jervis, John Rogerson, William Fownes and John Eccles, all immortalised in street names – had an obvious material interest in improving the port.

They did not stop there. As early as 1715, they turned their attention to the south shore and began the construction of what was eventually to become the Great South Wall. Work started on this heroic project as early as 1716. The Ballast Office showed great consistency of purpose over a long period of time in the face of formidable practical difficulties. A wall of timbered piles was first laid down, pushing out towards what is now the Poolbeg lighthouse. By 1731, the basic structure was complete from the Pigeon House to the Poolbeg. A light-ship marked the eastern end of the piles. All in all, it was a rickety and unsatisfactory structure. The disturbance of wind and tides was often too much for the timber wall. Individual piles were displaced and the constant maintenance requirements were onerous. Moreover, the uncertain mooring of the lightship presented a near insoluble problem.

This is turn raised the question of a permanent lighthouse as the only effective substitute. The Ballast Office first proposed it in 1736. The idea got nowhere; it was raised again in 1744 with similar results. It was not until 1759 that the piles themselves were acknowledged to be an inadequate solution and the decision was taken to build a stone wall. The design incorporated a provision for a lighthouse foundation at the eastern end.

The abutment for the lighthouse foundation was built first and then construction of the wall proceeded from east to west, or back towards the city. It took over thirty years to carry the wall all the way up to the site of the present O'Connell Bridge but the lighthouse was finished and functioning as early as 1767.

The Great South Wall is not simply one of the finest engineering and construction achievements in the city's history. It is a testimony to the tenacity of purpose and consistency of vision of the city authorities through the entire length of the eighteenth century. A project that was a gleam in the eye in 1716 was not completed until the 1790s, by which time the Ballast Office, the original sponsoring body, had been replaced by a new Ballast Board (1786) and no one alive at the start had survived to see it finished. It is in its way as splendid a memorial of the city's golden age as any Georgian square or municipal building.

The final enclosing wall in Dublin bay, the Bull Wall from Clontarf to the green North Bull Lighthouse, was first proposed in 1786. In the way of these things, it was not begun until 1819 and took five years to construct. It had two effects, one intended and the other not. The intended effect was to create a pincer in the bay, to narrow the navigation channel by bringing the Bull Wall to a

A depiction of Dublin, looking southward, made by Charles Brooking in 1728. It shows the lines of the South and East walls and ships at anchor in Ringsend.

A MAP of the CITY and Suburbs of DUBLIN And also the ARCH BISHOP and FAR

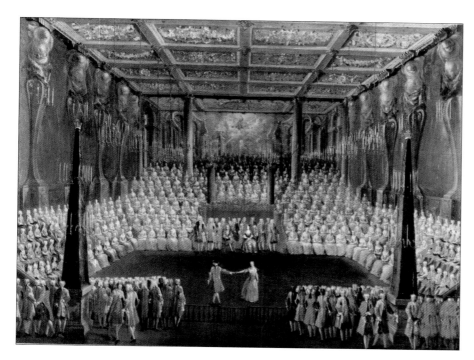

A state ball in all its glittering finery in Dublin Castle, painted by William van der Hagen in 1731.

point opposite to the Poolbeg lighthouse and thus creating what was hoped would be a self-scouring and dredging system as the tides ebbed and flowed. This ambition was largely fulfilled, with the ebb tides being especially important in this regard. Even before the wall was completed, the depth of water over the bar had increased by up to nine feet.

The unexpected consequence was that the North Bull sandbank in the lee of the new wall began to stand proud at high tide and form itself into the Bull Island. The process was first noticed in the 1820s, almost as soon as the wall was completed. Instead of sand being washed into the harbour itself, it was now retained by the wall, thus adding to the existing bank. It grew in the course of the nineteenth century, by the end of which it was almost 5 kms in extent and 6 metres above high water at its highest point. It accommodates two 18-hole

ATHS Liberties with the bounds of each PARISH Drawn from an Actual SURVEY

courses – Royal Dublin (1889) and St Anne's (1921) – and is one of the country's most important bird and wildlife sanctuaries. On the seaward side, its beach – named Dollymount for the nearest suburb – is a major public amenity, by far the most splendid beach within the city boundary. All this barely 7 kms from College Green!

One of the quaint features of the Bull Island is the wooden bridge that gives access to it at the city end. It stands on wooden piles and joins the landward abutment to the wall proper about 100 metres away. The purpose was to allow a clear tidal flow along the creek that lay to the landward of the North Bull sandbank (and later island). Known as Sutton Creek, this had for centuries afforded a place of shelter and relative safety for shipping in unfavourable conditions. The building of the later solid causeway (1964) as a second access to the Bull Island (about 2 kms to the east of the wooden bridge) without any such facility for flow-through reignited a controversy that still erupts from time to time. Happily, the wooden bridge is still there.

With the revival of the city's economic fortunes from the late seventeenth century on, wealthy and enterprising merchants and businessmen began to acquire parcels of land outside the walls with a view to property development. We have come across some of these from time to time before – men such as Sir Humphrey Jervis – but none were more influential than the three generations of the Gardiner family. The patriarch, Luke Gardiner (d. 1755), was a banker

In this watercolour, the Speaker enters the Irish House of Commons, led by the mace-bearer.

who married into the aristocratic Mountjoy family. It was he who oversaw the early development of the Gardiner estate in the north-east of the city during the first half of the century. His grandson, also Luke, Lord Mountjoy (1745–98: he was killed at the Battle of New Ross leading crown troops against the Wexford rebels) was the principal figure in the second half.

Luke Gardiner the Elder first developed the area at the northern end of Capel Street. Bolton Street dates from 1720 but the real triumph was Henrietta Street dating from a few years later. Here Gardiner built enormous town houses, vastly more spacious than anything else put up in the Georgian era. The hallways alone are huge, bigger than the total floor area of many modern suburban houses. One of the first residents was Hugh Boulter, archbishop of Armagh, a key political and social figure of the day. Fashion – not least clerical fashion – followed him. Before long, Henrietta Street was known colloquially as Primate's Hill. It helped to establish the north-east suburbs of the city as the centre of early fashionable life. The drift of the beau monde to the south side did not start in earnest until the second half of the century.

This Luke Gardiner was also responsible for the development of Gardiner's Mall, later to mutate into Sackville Street and later again to O'Connell Street. When Gardiner acquired it, it was known as Drogheda Street (or Lane). This was named for Henry Moore, Earl of Drogheda, who is commemorated in Henry Street, Moore Street, Earl Street and Of Lane, all of which have survived. Gardiner widened it by knocking down many of the existing properties and creating a central mall that ran from what is now Parnell Street to the modern Spire. This central area was named Gardiner's Mall, the two parallel sides Sackville Street – named for Lionel Sackville, Duke of Dorset, lord lieutenant in the 1730s. The unwidened lower end retained the name Drogheda Street (thus giving the earl a full house, for the moment at least) until the extension of Sackville Street to the river in the 1780s. Meanwhile the lord lieutenant was further immortalised in Dorset Street, which was developed (but not by Gardiner) along the line of the old Drumcondra Lane, the traditional city exit to the north.

Shortly before his death, Luke Gardiner the Elder began the development of Rutland Square (now Parnell Square) which in time became a major centre of fashion, never more so than when Lord Charlemont built his town house in Portland stone – to distinguish it from the mere brick of the mansions adjacent – in the 1760s. It is now the Hugh Lane Gallery.

At the corner of Rutland Square nearest the top of Sackville Street, Bartholomew Mosse acquired four acres of land in 1748. Mosse was the proprietor of the Lying-In Hospital, the first dedicated maternity hospital in the world which he had founded in George's Lane (now South Great George's Street) three years earlier. On this site he planned to build a larger maternity

Silver-gilt mace, the symbol of authority of the old Irish House of Lords. This elegant silver work was made in Dublin around 1760.

hospital and he engaged Richard Cassels, a Huguenot from Hesse in Germany who had inherited the practice of Edward Lovett Pearce and established himself as the leading Dublin architect of the 1730s and '40s. Cassels did not live to see his design realised but it was completed by his pupil John Ensor. The Roto – a Dublin landmark ever since – opened on 8 December 1757.

The building is designed in a chaste, classical manner with one notable exception. The chapel is one of the few genuine examples of Baroque exuberance in the city and represents a riotous contrast to the sobriety of the main building. On the rest of the complex, Mosse planned a pleasure gardens – modelled on Vauxhall in London – and the rotunda building at the northern end which gives the whole complex its name. This building, which offered public entertainments, and the gardens were centres of fashionable life and sources of revenue for the hospital.

The first half of the eighteenth century saw an explosion of public building, some of the very highest quality. The new Parliament House opened to the design of Edward Lovett Pearce in the 1730s, although the additions by Gandon and others from the 1780s give the building its modern appearance. Pearce's original structure was one of classical purity and dramatic confidence.

Across the street, Trinity began to assume its modern form. The oldest surviving structure in the college, the Rubrics, dates from the first decade of the century. In the second, Thomas Burgh designed the Old Library. There are still prints that show it in the form in which Burgh left it, but its modern form derives from Deane and Woodward's addition of the sensational barrel-vaulted ceiling in the 1860s. It is an ironic thought that while modern planning laws might have spared us the "restoration" of Christ Church and St Patrick's cathedrals in the nineteenth century, they would also have robbed us of what one authority has described as "the finest secular interior in Ireland".

Trinity was a work in progress for most of the century. The Printing House – a pretty building in the style of a Doric temple, the work of Cassels – dates from 1734. The Dining Hall followed in the next decade. The 1750s brought the great west front of the college giving onto College Green. Front Square itself was gradually completed in the 1780s. The Provost's House (1759) is the only private Georgian house in Dublin that still serves its original function.

Civic institutions of all kinds were founded in what was a display of growing urban self-possession. Jervis Street hospital started life as the Charitable Infirmary (1718) in Cook Street before eventually settling in its eponymous location in 1796, where it stayed until it closed in 1987. St Patrick's Hospital was endowed by proceeds from Jonathan Swift's will – he died in 1745 – and opened in 1757. It was the first psychiatric facility in Ireland and only the second in the British Isles. Swift himself had summarised its provenance and purpose in a verse:

He gave the little wealth he had
To build a home for fools and mad
And showed with one satiric touch
No nation need it so much.

The Tholsel, Dublin. This illustration, by James Malton, is reputed to be the best representation of the building that once stood in Skinner's Row, just south of Christ Church Cathedral.

The Dublin Society – later the Royal Dublin Society (RDS) – dates from 1731. The full title was the Dublin Society for the Improvement of Husbandry, Manufacturing and other Useful Arts. It was founded by fourteen gentlemen of learning, of whom Thomas Prior was the most notable. It was a typical product of the early Enlightenment: a voluntary association of private members, dedicated to the rational improvement of the applied arts. The term "practical idealism" is usually employed as an empty cant phrase but it seems completely appropriate here. The RDS's direct contribution to the life of the city is most easily set out in a list of the subsidiary entities established under its aegis: the Botanic Gardens (1795); Dublin's first school of art (1740s); its first museum

The West Front of Trinity College.

Jonathan Swift, 1667–1749.

(1790s), the remote ancestor of the National Museum of Ireland; the Natural History Museum; and the National Library of Ireland (1877), whose founding collection was based in large part upon the library of the RDS which was transferred to the new institution.

The RDS's original purpose, to speed agricultural improvement, still finds a bi-annual echo in its Spring Show and Horse Show, the latter for many generations one of the highlights of the city's social calendar.

Five years after the foundation of the RDS, the city had its first newspaper, the *Dublin Daily Advertiser*, but it was not until the first publication of the *Freeman's Journal* in 1763 that the city acquired a continuous journalistic voice.

We have mentioned Jonathan Swift only in passing, but no overview of Dublin in the first half of the eighteenth century is complete without him. He was born in Dublin in 1667. Both parents were English, although his maternal grandparents had themselves lived in Ireland in the 1630s. Swift's father was an official in the King's Inns in Dublin. The family was well connected: they were related to the Duke of Ormond on Swift's mother's side and were close to the Master of the Rolls in London, Sir John Temple, whose son, Sir William Temple, would become Jonathan Swift's influential patron as a young man. He was also related to John Dryden, the leading English poet of the age.

The Swifts were therefore typical of many English families that established themselves in Dublin following the Restoration – the Ormond connection, in particular, would have done them no harm – and prospered with the developing city. The elder Swift died a few months before his son was born but the family memory of persecution by the Puritans in Cromwell's time – what Swift himself described as "the barbarity of Cromwell's hellish crew" – inclined them towards an orthodox mainstream Anglicanism. This was the tradition into which Jonathan Swift was born. He was educated at Kilkenny grammar school, a preferred academy of the Old English since pre-Reformation times and by now a reliable centre of Church of Ireland conformity. He was ordained in the church in 1695.

He was an ambitious clergyman and his ambition was firmly fixed on the larger island. In the first decade of the eighteenth century, he was in London and was an influential figure in literary and political circles. He wrote for *The Tatler*, and was a friend of Pope and other leading wits and writers. Politically, he hitched his star to the Tories under Harley and Bolinbroke, but the death of Queen Anne ushered in the long Whig hegemony and Tory sympathisers were out of favour. Swift had backed the wrong horse. Instead of an appointment to the bench of bishops in the Church of England, which he had hoped for, he was returned to Dublin as a mere dean, albeit Dean of St Patrick's cathedral.

For Swift, this was exile. He had harboured thoughts, not unreasonably, of a glittering career in the metropolis – the greatest city in Europe except for Paris – but had to settle for provincial Dublin instead. The ripening of Swift's satirical genius had this background for context. The Swifts were nominally Irish, but really English in Ireland and thinly rooted there. And the patriotism that Jonathan Swift was to espouse and personify from the 1720s was that of the frustrated provincial, the creole abandoned by the metropole, condescended to and dismissed as of lesser account. Much of what was denominated patriotism in the eighteenth century – culminating in Grattan's Parliament in the last two decades – was of this kind. When an existential threat to this settler community arose in the wake of the French Revolution, the façade collapsed with suggestive ease.

None the less, the fact that a truculent colonial patriotism did develop was a testimony to the increasingly confident position of the New English elite in

A Georgian doorway.

the early eighteenth century. They represented barely 10 per cent of the Irish population; they were observant Church of Ireland in their confessional allegiance, surrounded by a sea of Catholics and – in their Ulster redoubt – Presbyterians. In a manner typical of pre-industrial states, this elite alone constituted the political nation. Their victory in the Williamite wars at the end of the preceding century had delivered them the security that made their position seem impregnable. This sense of security was the essential condition for their patriotism, because a nervous or insecure community could not have afforded the luxury of anti-English sentiment.

And of that sentiment, there was no shortage. The colonial parliament chafed under restrictions on its discretionary powers that dated from medieval times. Such restrictions were perfectly usual in provincial or subordinate assemblies in pre-modern Europe but they were a source of tension none the less. In Ireland, this tension was increased in 1720 by the passage of the Declaratory Act in London, which stated that Westminster could pass legislation binding on Ireland over the head of the Dublin parliament. Then came the controversy known as Wood's Halfpence.

William Wood was an ironmaster in Wolverhampton, near Birmingham. In 1722, he was awarded a patent to mint £100,000 worth of copper coin for Ireland. This patent aroused immediate and spirited opposition in Ireland, where there was no national mint. It was alleged that he received the patent by paying £10,000 to the Duchess of Kendal, one of the king's mistresses. The total amount of currency in circulation in Ireland was about £400,000, so there was an understandable fear that Wood's coins would flood the country and cause a severe inflation.

That was the primary objection to the coinage, but there was also a sense of resentment that the Irish parliament had been bypassed yet again. The entire Irish establishment united against the coinage and refused to circulate it. In 1725, the London government admitted defeat and withdrew the patent. In the meantime, Swift had established himself as a master satirist by writing the six pamphlets collectively known as *The Drapier's Letters*. Assuming the disguise of M.B. Drapier, a respectable shopkeeper, Swift attacked the patent, but reserved his most acid and brilliant ridicule for the demeaning and subordinate position in which the colonial parliament was held.

The letters were addressed quite self-consciously to a Protestant audience, in an age when Dublin was still a Protestant city. Swift should not be confused with the later tradition of patriotism in the Irish nationalist context of the nineteenth and twentieth centuries. There was a common anti-English sentiment, but there the similarities end. Swift would almost certainly have been a unionist in the nineteenth century: the vast majority of the descendants of those he addressed in his satires were. Where he does represent the beginning of a tradition, however, is in the literary sense. He is the first in a line of Irish – usually Dublin – writers who have, whether in Ireland or overseas, been the island's glory. He stands at the head of a great tradition, one of the writers of true world importance that the city has produced.

By the mid century, Dublin had a population of about 150,000. It had grown to be the largest city in Britain or Ireland apart from London. It was an era of peace, expanding commerce and physical expansion. The early pre-eminence of the north side was gradually reversed. The key moment in this was the decision by the Duke of Leinster – Ireland's only duke – to locate his town house in the south-east quarter. The building of Leinster House had exactly the effect that the duke had predicted: fashion followed him south. Within a few years, Merrion Square was being laid out and the city was assuming its modern shape. While the north side did not lose its social cachet until the nineteenth century,

the south side was now firmly established as the more fashionable quarter. It has never lost that status.

The contrasts that are characteristic of any city at any time were never far away. In 1740 and 1741, there were bread riots in Dublin, as the whole island was gripped by a famine which proportionally was probably more severe than the Great Famine of the 1840s. It is estimated that up to 400,000 people died of starvation and consequent illnesses in these years, out of a total population of about 2.5 million. But just a year later, in 1742, Dublin played host to one of the great first performances in the history of European music. On 13 April, under the direction of the composer, Handel's *Messiah* was first performed in the New Musick Hall in Fishamble Street.

Such were the opposites typical of eighteenth-century European societies: on the one hand, the desperate subsistence crisis; on the other, ducal magnificence and artistic triumph. For by now, Dublin was truly reckoned to be a major European city. One visitor in the 1730s calculated that only London, Paris, Rome and Amsterdam had greater populations. He might have added Naples and a few others, but the general point was valid. By the mid-century, Dublin was established in the front rank of European cities.

Leinster House, designed by Richard Cassels for the Earl of Kildare, as completed around 1745. Later it would become the Dublin Society Library.

Hallelujah

1685 was a good year for European music, for in that year were born Johann Sebastian Bach, Domenico Scarlatti and Georg Friedrich Handel. Handel, who was to outlive the other two, showed early evidence of his genius and had two operas in production in Germany by the time he was twenty. At the age of twenty-five, he was appointed kappelmeister or music director to the Elector of Hanover, soon to be the first of the Hanoverian line of English monarchs when he assumed the throne in 1714 as King George I.

Handel followed him to London. There the young composer became director of the Royal Academy of Music and the composer of many operas. Following an illness and some financial setbacks in the late 1730s, Handel concentrated thereafter on sacred oratorio.

In 1741, he received an invitation to visit Dublin from the Lord Lieutenant of Ireland, the duke of Devonshire. Handel's music was already well known and popular with Dublin audiences, although the prevailing city fashion was for knockabout ballad opera. It would be wrong to propose early Georgian Dublin as more sophisticated than it actually was. The invitation was a welcome development at a time when Handel was uncertain of his future and was considering a permanent return to Germany. Instead, his life and the history of music took a turn for the better. He was asked to compose an oratorio to be given in Dublin in support of some city charities. The result was *Messiah*, with a libretto by Charles Jennens based on Biblical texts.

The oratorio was composed in London in August and September 1741. In late October, he set out for Dublin via Chester. The winds were contrary, however, and Handel employed the resultant delay in departure to rehearse parts of *Messiah* with local singers. He eventually reached Dublin on 18 November and took lodgings in Abbey Street.

Shortly before Handel's arrival, a new concert venue opened in Dublin. Neale's New Musick Hall in Fishamble Street, in the very oldest part of the city, was the venue for a series of subscription concerts which Handel gave that winter: from Christmas 1741 to the following April, they performed to enthusiastic and appreciative audiences. Then, on 13 April 1742, at the same venue, *Messiah* was given in public for the first time. An audience of over 700 turned up to a venue whose normal capacity was 600. To accommodate the crush, gentlemen were asked not to wear their swords, nor ladies their hoops.

It was a triumph. The charities in whose name the performance was given benefited handsomely and *Messiah* went on to become one of the world's best-loved pieces of sacred music. Of its most famous passage, the *Hallelujah Chorus*,

Handel himself wrote: "Whether I was in my body or out of my body as I wrote it I know not. God knows."

Handel gave other performances in Dublin. He conducted *Saul* on 25 May and repeated *Messiah* on 3 June. He left the city on 13 August, probably intending to return. But he never did. His fortunes in London revived dramatically, with the enthusiastic reception it gave to *Messiah* and – even more so – to *Samson*.

His memory has never left Dublin. The New Musick Hall went the way of all flesh, to be replaced by Kennan's Ironworks. But on this site, every 13 April since 1989, Our Lady's Choral Society perform excerpts from *Messiah*. The springtime weather in Dublin can often be unkind, with vicious April showers. Nothing daunted, the choir pays its annual tribute – come hail or shine – to a glorious moment in the history of the city.

Members of Our Lady's Choral Society caught in an April shower as they perform excerpts from Messiah *at the site of the original New Musick Hall.*

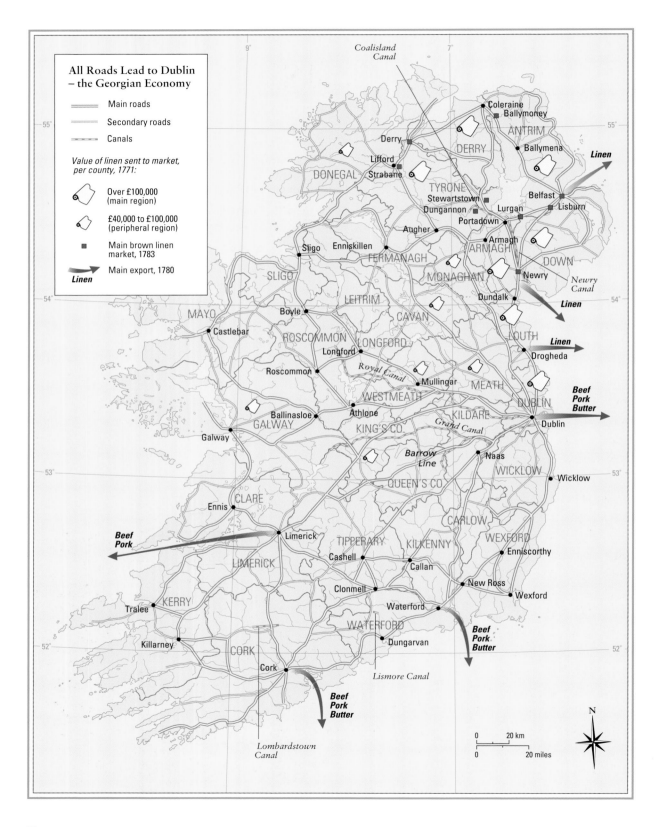

All Roads Lead to Dublin
– the Georgian Economy

Main roads

Secondary roads

Canals

*Value of linen sent to market,
per county, 1771:*

Over £100,000
(main region)

£40,000 to £100,000
(peripheral region)

Main brown linen
market, 1783

Linen   Main export, 1780

CHAPTER 7
GEORGIANS

The establishment of the Wide Streets Commissioners in 1757 was the most enlightened piece of planning legislation the city's history. The body it set up was charged with widening existing narrow streets and proposing standards for new ones. It was empowered to buy land and property where necessary. The Commissioners – there were usually 25 in number – were all men of substance and influence. What they created was a city re-imagined as an aristocratic display space, no longer simply the random, twisting pattern of streets dictated by ancient pathways and commercial necessity.

The modern city is unimaginable without their work. All the classic Georgian squares and streets on both side of the river felt their influence. Merrion Square is the prime example: the view along the south side of the square and down Upper Mount Street to the perspective point of the Peppercannister church is the best formal testimony to their purpose. But every district felt their influence. They had real powers – they could override the Corporation in those areas within their remit – and they did not hesitate to use them.

They widened Lower Sackville Street down to the river and on the far side of Carlisle (now O'Connell) Bridge created the triangle of D'Olier Street, College Street and Westmoreland Street. They built Parliament Street to give better access to the Castle and widened Skinner's Row, one of the narrowest choke points in the old city, to create Christchurch Place. Dame Street owes its width to them. Oddly, they did not join the top of Dame Street to Christchurch Place, preferring instead to retain the narrow Castle Street link that survived from medieval times. Lord Edward Street, which filled this lacuna, was not punched through until the 1880s. On the approaches to the city, Baggot Street, Dorset Street and James's Street all owe their width to the Commissioners.

Medallion of the 1st Ulster Regiment, Irish Volunteers.

The remarkable formal unity of Georgian Dublin is a product of the Wide Streets Commissioners work. The great squares – Merrion and Fitzwilliam on the south side and Rutland (now Parnell) and Mountjoy on the north – plus their surrounding streets are clearly part of a common architectural vision. Even the north-side streets and squares, much reduced in beauty by a century of decay, neglect and vandalism, still bear testimony to that vision. The effect was to girdle the old city with a series of rectilinear processional and leisure spaces on its eastern and northern margins, with a visual consistency that is the city's thumbprint.

The new city was to be embraced by the arms of two canals. On the south side, the Grand Canal was started in the 1750s. It linked Dublin to the River Shannon and also provided the city with an enhanced supply of potable water from two holding basins in the suburbs. The first commercial traffic started in 1779 and a passenger service began the following year. The company built a series of hotels along the route. By the end of the century, the canal had linked to the mouth of the Liffey at Ringsend and the Grand Canal Dock was built.

On the north side, the Royal Canal was not completed until 1817, the first barge having sailed in 1806. It was never as successful as the Grand and its later arrival left it even more vulnerable to the railway revolution in the mid nineteenth century.

The classical eighteenth-century city was contained within the arms of the canals, with the Victorian suburban developments of the next century spread-

Looking up the River Liffey, c. 1796. This watercolour by James Malton shows the Marine School on the south bank which eventually became a storage depot and was finally demolished in the twentieth century.

ing beyond them. Shadowing the canals and running in rough parallel to them, the North and South Circular Roads date from the 1760s. One aspect of the Grand Canal was the branch extension that ran from Goldenbridge in the western suburbs into the back of James's Street, to service the new brewery at St James's Gate. This was Guinness, the most famous commercial product ever developed in the city, which dated from 1759.

The same year saw the completion of one of the city's other landmarks, the great West Front of Trinity facing onto College Green. By now, St Stephen's Green was fully developed, with the north side (Beaux Walk) being especially fashionable. The west side was less so, due to the presence of a gallows near the corner of Cuffe Street, a reminded of how physically close were the beau monde and the demi monde in an eighteenth-century city. A further physical survivor from the era prior to the development of the Green stands at the north-east corner, at the start of Merrion Row. The Huguenot Cemetery dates from 1693, when it would have been in an obscure, out-of-the-way location. However, it has maintained a continuous presence there ever since, although the last interment was in 1901. The lintel stone over the gate contains the most visible mis-spelling in the city, announcing the place as the Hughenot [sic] cemetery.

The story of eighteenth-century Dublin is usually told in terms similar to this narrative so far. It is the era of classical and aristocratic swagger, of heroic building projects, of the triumph of rational, enlightenment town planning. And yes, it was all those things. But there was a dark face as well. Don't forget that gallows near Cuffe Street.

There was no city police force. Instead, there were a series of parish watches established under Act of Parliament of 1723. Under local parish direction, these watches employed constables and watchmen to patrol the parish in the hours of darkness. In extremis, they could call on military support from the Castle as a back-up, but in general they were on their own. Nor were they in any way co-ordinated across parish boundaries, which criminals could therefore cross safely in the knowledge that they were in the clear.

Dublin was a violent city. Robbery, especially after dark, was a constant threat and pickpockets were ubiquitous. Beggars and vagrants were everywhere: the contrast between ascendancy style and the destitute poor was stark, as in much of the modern Third World. The English wit Samuel Foote, on a visit to the city, said that he had never known what English beggars did with their cast-off rags until he saw Irish beggars.

Sectarian rioting was a commonplace. The Liberty Boys – mainly Protestant weavers from the Liberties near St Patrick's cathedral – fought regularly with the Ormond Boys – mostly Catholic butchers from the market on the north shore of the river. The whole summer of 1748 was given over to a series of af-

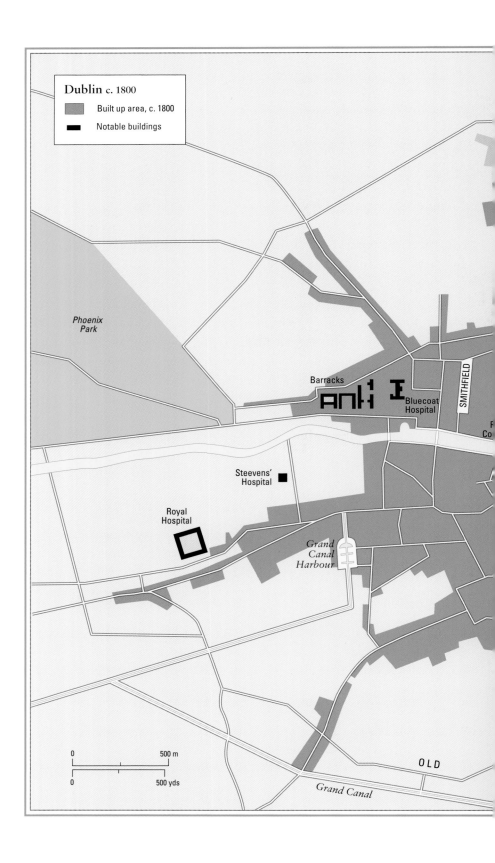

Dublin c. 1800

Built up area, c. 1800

Notable buildings

Phoenix
Park

Barracks

Bluecoat
Hospital

SMITHFIELD

Steevens'
Hospital

Royal
Hospital

Grand
Canal
Harbour

OLD

Grand Canal

0   500 m

0   500 yds

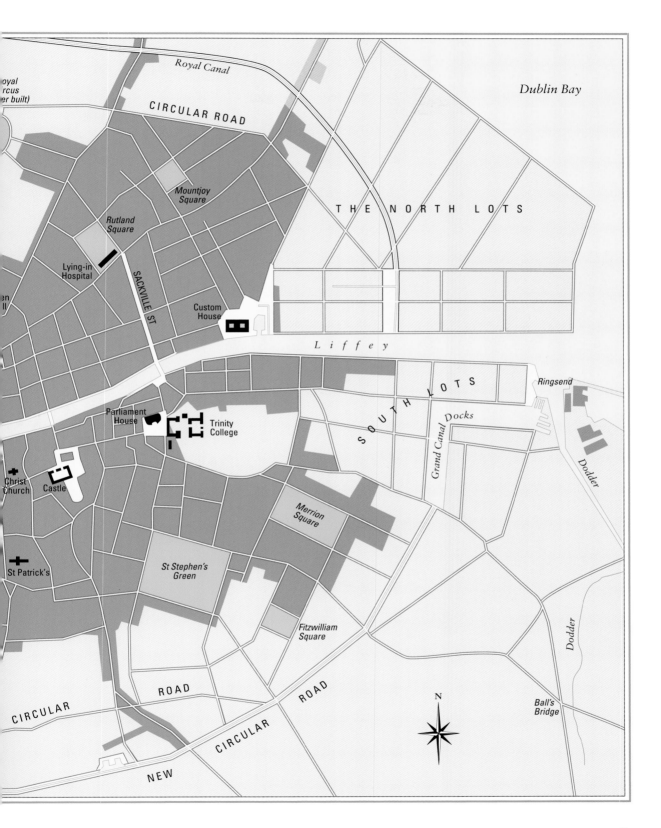

frays, many of them extremely violent and entailing horrendous injuries and fatalities. Although eventually suppressed by the city authorities at the end of that summer, riots between the factions continued to punctuate the rest of the century without ever again attaining the fervour of that year.

Public holidays and fairs were also likely to be occasions of drunken rioting. The notorious Donnybrook Fair – originally sanctioned by royal charter as far back as 1204 – had long since become one such. Essentially a horse fair, by the eighteenth century it had attracted various other forms of commerce, not the least of which was prostitution. In this connection, the city was very adequately stocked and had been for a long time. In the early seventeenth century, Barnabe Rich, the English soldier and author, complained that "every filthy alehouse [has] a number of young, idle housewives that are very loathsome, filthy and abominable, both in life and manners, and these they call tavern-keepers, the most of them known harlots". Even earlier, we know of the location of certain brothels, one in particular being at the Bagnio Slip (the modern Fownes Street in Temple Bar). A bagnio was ostensibly a washhouse, but usually the term was used to disguise a brothel, as in this case. The facility in question survived into the eighteenth century.

A Georgian doorway.

Attitudes to prostitution depended largely on the disposition of individual magistrates. The severity of the more moral (or moralising) was counter-pointed by instances in which judicial leniency could best and most plausibly be explained by the bench having prior acquaintance of the ladies arraigned before them. There were many instances of men being murdered in brothels, either by rivals or in some instances by the women themselves. Such incidents could lead to wholesale rioting, as in the case of Smock Alley in 1768. This street between Christ Church cathedral and the river was home to the city's most famous theatre. It also contained, not entirely coincidentally in an age when actresses and prostitutes were thought to be one and the same, the greatest concentration of bawdy houses. The 1768 riots went on for the best part of a week, resulted in the wholesale wrecking of suspected premises, and were only finally quelled by cavalry.

Brothels were ubiquitous in Dublin but the area around Christchurch was the focus of the trade. In Copper Alley, next to Smock Alley, a notorious brothel keeper, Darkey Kelly, was convicted in 1764 of murdering one of his clients and was burnt alive in the still half developed Stephen's Green, within shouting distance of the fashionable Beaux Walk.

Mention of Beaux Walk is a reminder that crime and dissipation were not just the province of the the poor. Dublin still had some of the air of a new-money frontier town, whose aristocracy was of recent establishment and accordingly coarse in its tastes. Dublin's "Bucks" – young men of fashion and wealth much given to drunken dissipation, gambling and riot – were, in their own way, leaders of contemporary urban style. The most famous was Thomas "Buck" Whaley, son of the MP Richard Chapell Whaley. The elder Whaley was a notorious religious bigot, who had to endure (or enjoy) the punning sobriquet "Burn Chapel" in the light of his hatred and harassment of Catholics. Like many a bad man, he did well out of public life and left his son a fortune when he died in 1769.

The boy – he was only three when his father died – wasted little time in blowing his inheritance. He followed his father into parliament at the age of eighteen but spent most of his time at the gaming tables in the nearby Daly's

The Casino at Marino, designed by William Chambers as a summer house for Lord Charlemont, is the most perfect piece of neo-classical architecture in Ireland.

Club, the resort of choice for the jeunesse dorée of the day. He continued to run through his money when he went to Paris and was forced back to Ireland. He won a bet by leaping out of the first-floor window of his palatial house at no. 86 St Stephen's Green straight into a waiting coach below. His most famous wager was reputedly for the colossal sum of £20,000, to win which he had to travel to Jerusalem and back in less than two years. He did it in nine months, an astonishing

achievement in eighteenth-century travelling conditions. Of course, it made him famous. According to the charming but unreliable diarist Jonah Barrington, he took bribes from both sides to vote for and against the Act of Union. Barrington did the same thing himself.

It is one of the city's minor historical ironies that the Buck's great house, bequeathed him by his Papist-baiting father, passed into the hands of the Church of Rome in the 1850s and became the first home of the new Catholic University, the antecedent to University College Dublin. It was renamed Newman House in honour of the cardinal who was the presiding founder of the university.

There were many other celebrated Bucks, not to mention the notoriously rowdy and lawless Trinity students who were effectively above the law, being granted a sort of tribal indulgence denied to their less fortunate fellow-townsmen. In a sense, the ferocity of the punishments meted out to the criminal classes – the hangings, burnings, pillories, transportation, whippings (whether at whipping posts or through the streets) – were a distorting mirror for the excesses of the cosseted elite. The behaviour of the latter was as brutal in its way as the punishments of the courts. The temper of Georgian Dublin, once you got a little under the glittering surface, was nervous, raw and provincial.

Take the case of Tiger Roche, another celebrated hearty. He was born in

The western approaches to the city as delineated in John Rocque's detailed map of 1756.

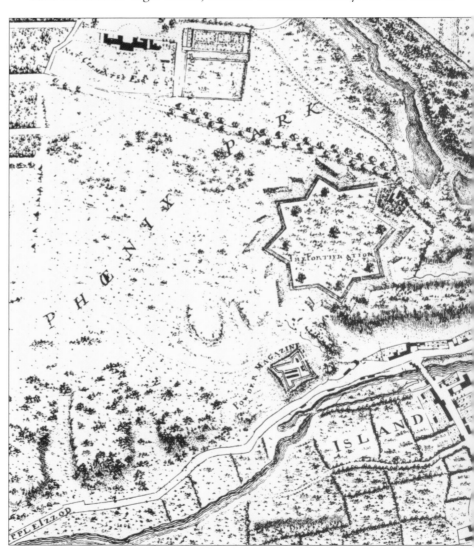

1729. He showed enough promise as a young man to attract the good opinion of Lord Chesterfield, the celebrated essayist who was Lord Lieutenant of Ireland at the time. But he soon fell into rakish company, got involved in a drunken affray and killed a night watchman. He fled to America and fought with the French in the Indian wars. He was wrongly convicted of stealing a gun from a fellow officer, and promptly attacked his prison guard by sinking his teeth into the unfortunate's throat. On his return to England, he made it his life's mission to seek out and harm all who had testified against him. Back in Dublin, he formed a vigilante group to counter a criminal gang known as the pinkindindies, whose speciality was "pinking", that is slashing, its victims with half-hidden swords prior to robbing them.

These pinkindindies are further evidence of the precarious nature of law

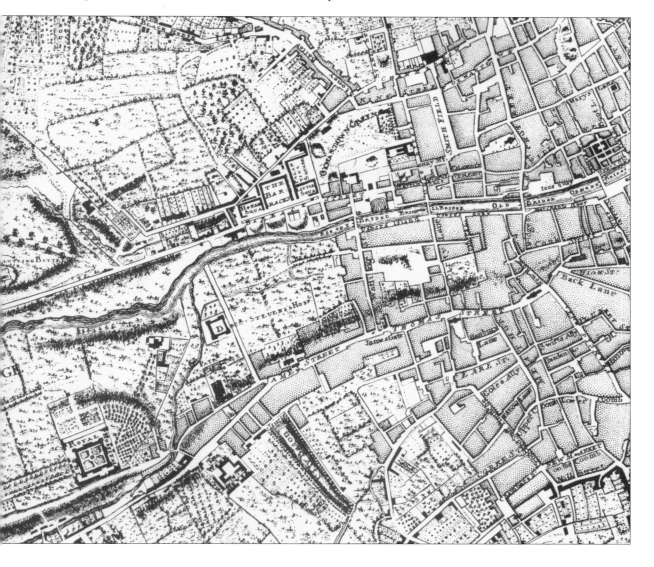

and order in Georgian Dublin. They were gentlemen scoundrels – ergo the swords – very often looking to recoup gambling losses or other products of improvidence from the unarmed innocent. Roche subsequently went to London, married money and spent it, and then got an army commission in India. There he quarrelled with a fellow officer who was subsequently murdered. Although Roche was tried for the crime, he was twice acquitted on insufficient evidence before disappearing from history.

If it were possible to travel back in time, the first thing that would strike any modern person transported to an eighteenth-century city would be the smell. There were no sewers. Waste, whether human faeces or dirty water generally, was collected in cesspits. These were cylindrical tanks dug into the earth and filled with refuse. They were covered and required to be emptied on a regular basis as they filled up. Each house had its own cesspit and the aggregate effect, especially in warm summer weather, was overpowering. Moreover, the pits attracted flies and vermin. It is hardly to be wondered that the rich fled to the country for the summer to escape the stink.

Dublin was no different to anywhere else in this regard. As late as 1853, George Halpin, the inspector of works for the Ballast Board, declared that "the Liffey is still the great main drain into which the sewerage of Dublin opens". Scavengers and night soil men (shit collectors who either dumped their cargo in the river or sold it on for fertiliser) were employed by the city authorities to keep the cesspits serviced and the streets otherwise as clean as possible.

There were other hazards. The city was dark at night, facilitating the various criminal elements who preyed on the unwary. A system of public lanterns in the city centre, maintained at the residents' expense, was gradually developed but it was a very partial answer to a larger problem, the real solution of which had to await the development of the electric light in the next century.

Fire was a constant concern, especially in the older parts of the city which still contained a great number of wooden buildings. A primitive fire fighting service dates from 1706 and the earliest fire insurance scheme from 1740, at which time fire insurance was well established in Britain.

In all, the Georgian city was a place of violent contrasts. It was still, in every sense, a work in progress. When the Dublin parliament gained "legislative independence" from Westminster in 1782, there was as yet no Custom House or Four Courts or Fitzwilliam or Mountjoy Squares. There was a primitive piped water system, no main drainage or proper street lighting and a sub-culture of violence common to bucks and criminals alike, unchallenged by a municipal police force. Many of these absences were simply a product of their time and were common to all of Europe. Some were, in whole or in part, due to Dublin's relative newness as a significant city.

Arthur

In the 1750s, Mark Rainsford, later to be Lord Mayor of Dublin, owned a disused brewery at St James's Gate on the western approach to the city of Dublin. Rainsford's name is still commemorated in a street name in the district. His old brewery stood on twenty-four acres and comprised, inter alia, "a dwelling-house, a brewhouse, two malt houses, and stables". In 1759, he found a buyer.

Arthur Guinness had been born in Celbridge, Co. Kildare, about 15 kilometres west of the city, in 1725. In 1756 he had leased a brewery in nearby Leixlip, but the St James's Gate property gave him the chance to set up in the city. On the last day of 1759, he signed a 9,000-year lease on the premises at £45 per annum.

Guinness was a liberal in politics and a supporter of Henry Grattan, perhaps not unconnected to the fact that Grattan was a proponent of low excise taxes. He was also in favour of Catholic relief, but was opposed to the United Irishmen. For this his principal product was called "Guinness's black Protestant porter", the term black Protestant being used by overheated Catholics to describe what they regarded as bigots on the other side. On any reading of Guinness's politics, the smear is unfair albeit witty.

At first Guinness brewed ale at St James's Gate, as he had done in Leixlip. But in 1778 he moved on to porter. This black beer, brewed from dark malts, took its name from its popularity with London market porters, it having first been developed in that city. In due course a stronger black brew, twice the alcoholic volume of porter, acquired the name stout. From 1799, Guinness brewed only porter as his enterprise expanded.

His grandson, Sir Benjamin Lee Guinness (1798-1868), was the key figure in the huge expansion of the brewery during the nineteenth century. He developed a big export trade to Britain and personally paid for the restoration of St Patrick's cathedral. By now, the family were very rich and very grand indeed. Sir Benjamin's son, Arthur Edward (1840-1915), was educated at Eton and became the first Lord Ardilaun. He continued his father's philanthropic ways, restoring Marsh's Library, donating generous funding to the Coombe maternity hospital and granting St Stephen's Green to the city as a public space in 1880.

For most of the twentieth century, Guinness was by far the biggest commercial enterprise in Dublin and a prized place of employment. At a time of generally shabby-genteel poverty in the city, a permanent position in the brewery brought both security and prestige. The brewery had a reputation as an exceptionally good if paternalistic employer. Labour troubles were unknown, employee welfare schemes were subsidised, and all under a management that was resolutely Protestant in the capital of the Catholic republic.

The novelist Flann O'Brien, in his *At Swim-Two-Birds*, a work of comic genius, describes the narrator's uncle in the following terms: "Red-faced, bead-eyed, ball-bellied. Fleshy around the shoulders with long swinging arms giving ape-like effect to gait. Large moustache. Holder of Guinness clerkship the third class." Not many respectable Guinness clerks would have recognised themselves in that description.

Perhaps it is O'Brien's other paean to Guinness that rings truest with all Dubliners. Later in the same book, he has Jem Casey, "the poet of the pick", deliver a piece of inspired doggerel in praise of Arthur's product under the title "The Workman's Friend". One stanza will suffice:

When things go wrong and will not come right,
Though you do the best you can,
When life looks black as the hour of night –
A PINT OF PLAIN IS YOUR ONLY MAN.

Guinness: the craft of the cooper. Coopering involves the manufacture of wooden casks. Guinness had its own team of coopers working on site producing casks which carried stout and porter to its customers throughout Ireland and around the world.

CHAPTER 8
THE OLD HOUSE ON COLLEGE GREEN

The following piece of verse circulated in Ireland in the early eighteenth century:

God save the king,
God save the faith's defender.
God save (no harm in saving)
The pretender.
But who pretender is and who the king,
God save us all
Now that's another thing.

The Protestant victory in the wars of the late seventeenth century seemed decisive. Indeed, they proved to be so, but were not so felt. The danger of a Jacobite restoration haunted the new elite, soon to be known as the ascendancy. It was not hysterical to suppose such a thing possible. The Glorious Revolution of 1689 which had run King James II out of his three kingdoms was an act of usurpation, a coup d'etat. On any calculation of legitimate regnal succession, James' descendants had a better claim to the throne than the Hanoverian dynasty that replaced them.

However, any Jacobite restoration would have imperilled the land settlement, which explains the nervousness expressed in the verse. For gentlemen unsteadily settled on their new estates, an each-way bet made some sense, in case they might have to accommodate themselves to a restored old regime. After all, there were two military attempts at a Stuart restoration in Scotland in the first half of the eighteenth century, in 1715 and 1745. Had success attended either effort, it is not possible to know what would have happened in England, but it was reasonable to infer that the Stuarts would have natural allies among the dispossessed Irish.

These fears were heightened by the fact that the major European Catholic powers, France in particular, continued to regard the Stuarts as the legitimate monarchs of England, Scotland and Ireland. Likewise, and unsurprisingly, so did the Vatican. The siege mentality that this induced in the early ascendancy

Opposite: *Edward Lovett Pearce's Parliament House on College Green, built in the 1730s, was one of the great triumphs of public architecture in eighteenth-century Dublin.*

accounts for much of the formal ferocity of the anti-Catholic (and anti-Dissenter) Penal Laws.

As the century wore on, these fears gradually abated. The Hanoverian dynasty seemed ever more secure. But for as long as James II's son lived, the danger remained. Known to history as the Old Pretender, he would have become king in any Stuart restoration. It was in support of precisely that objective that his son, Charles Edward (Bonnie Prince Charlie or the Young Pretender) had mounted the '45 in Scotland that had ended in the slaughter at Culloden and the prince's romantic flight back to France and later Italy, there to live out his days in an alcoholic stupor.

The Old Pretender died in 1766, at which point the papacy decided that the game was up. Pope Clement XIII regarded the Stuarts as a busted flush, declined to give the Young Pretender the same recognition as his late father and instead formally acknowledged the Hanoverian George III as the legitimate king. The final removal of this external threat had the effect of making ascendancy interests even more secure in their historic triumph.

But security breeds another kind of confidence, the kind that allows for internal dissentions that had been suppressed in times of greater danger. The emergence of the so-called patriot interest in the Irish parliament in the last third of the century was no coincidence. Patriotism has often been called "colonial nationalism". It represented a sensibility among some members of the ascendancy that Irish colonial interests had been subordinated to English interests, and that the larger kingdom had been oppressive and selfish in its dealings with the smaller.

Restrictions on the Irish cattle and woollen trades were resented, as was the regular practice of awarding plum positions in church and state to English candidates rather than Irish. Parliament itself was subordinate to Westminster. The argument was made that Ireland was a separate kingdom which should be ruled by her own people (meaning the Anglican elite who alone constituted the political nation in a pre-democratic age). These sentiments had been present throughout the century – the Wood's Halfpence affair being the best example from an earlier generation – but the growing self-assurance of the ascendancy as a whole gave them renewed oxygen.

Benjamin Franklin visited Ireland in 1771 and found among the Irish patriots men of a similar temper to those Americans who chafed under British colonial exactions. When the American Revolution broke out four years later, it found ready support among ascendancy radicals. They forced the London government to abolish Irish export restrictions, so long a cause of tension between the two sides. The London government pulled regular troops out of Ireland to fight in America, leaving the country under-protected. Into this gap flowed a newly-formed Irish Volunteer force which began to mobilise in 1778. It was an entirely Protestant body under landlord leadership and by 1779, it numbered about 40,000 members. This number increased by a half to 60,000 by 1782. It proved to be a powerful persuader for further concessions from London. In

A muster of Volunteers in College Green in the later 1770s.

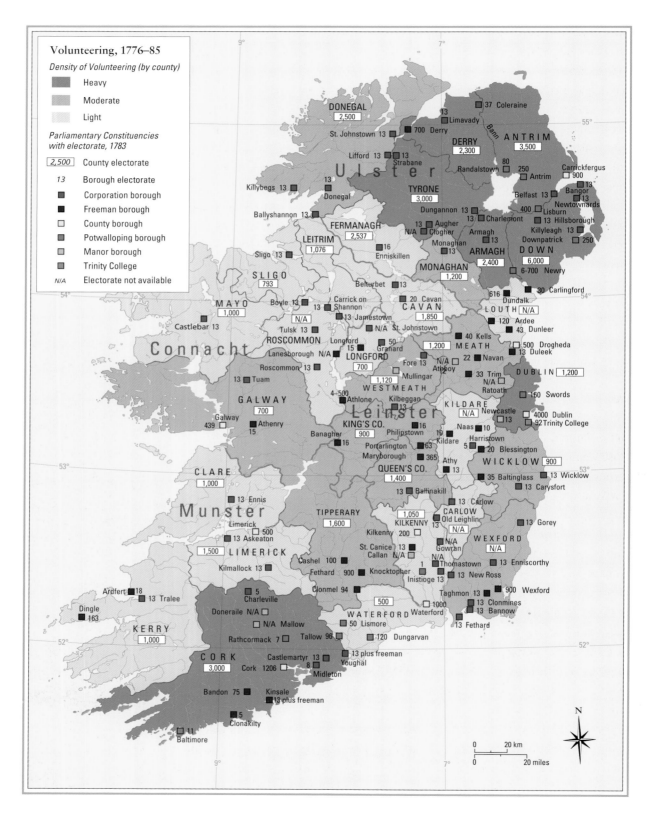

Volunteering, 1776–85

Density of Volunteering (by county)

- Heavy
- Moderate
- Light

Parliamentary Constituencies with electorate, 1783

- 2,500   County electorate
- 13   Borough electorate
- Corporation borough
- Freeman borough
- County borough
- Potwalloping borough
- Manor borough
- Trinity College
- N/A   Electorate not available

DONEGAL 2,500

St. Johnstown 13

13 Limavady   37 Coleraine

700 Derry

DERRY 2,300

ANTRIM 3,500

Lifford 13   13 Strabane

Randalstown   80   250   Carrickfergus

U l s t e r

Antrim

900

Killybegs 13   13   Donegal

TYRONE 3,000

Belfast 13   Bangor 13

Dungannon 13

Ballyshannon 13

FERMANAGH 2,537

400   Lisburn   Newtownards

13 Charlemont   13 Hillsborough

13 Augher

N/A   Clogher

Armagh   Killyleagh

LEITRIM 1,076

Monaghan   13   Downpatrick   250

16

Sligo 13

Enniskillen

MONAGHAN 1,200

ARMAGH 2,400

D O W N 6,000

6-700 Newry

Belturbet 13

616   Dundalk

30 Carlingford

S L I G O 793

Carrick on   20 Cavan

Boyle 13   13   Shannon

L O U T H   N/A

120 Ardee

M A Y O 1,000

13 Jamestown

CAVAN 1,850

43 Dunleer

Castlebar 13

Tulsk 13   N/A St. Johnstown

40 Kells

C o n n a c h t

Longford 50

Granard

M E A T H 1,200

N/A   500 Drogheda

13 Duleek

ROSCOMMON N/A

Lanesborough N/A

15

22 Navan

Roscommon 13

LONGFORD 700

Fore 13   N/A   Athboy

33 Trim

D U B L I N 1,200

13 Tuam

Mullingar

N/A   Ratoath

160 Swords

GALWAY 700

W E S T M E A T H 1,120

4-500   Athlone

Kilbeggan 13

K I L D A R E   N/A

Newcastle

Galway   Athenry

L e i n s t e r

4000 Dublin

439   15

KING'S CO. 900

Philipstown   19   Naas 10

13   92 Trinity College

Banagher

Kildare   5   Harristown

16

16

Portarlington 63   20 Blessington

Maryborough   365

Athy   W I C K L O W 900

QUEEN'S CO. 1,400

13   35 Baltinglass   13 Wicklow

C L A R E 1,000

13 Ballinakill   13 Carysfort

13 Ennis

13 Carlow

M u n s t e r

TIPPERARY 1,600

KILKENNY 1,050

Old Leighlin

13 Gorey

Limerick   500

CARLOW N/A

13 Askeaton

Kilkenny 200

W E X F O R D N/A

Kilmallock 13

St. Canice 13   Gowran

13 Enniscorthy

LIMERICK 1,500

Cashel 100   Callan N/A   1 Thomastown

Fethard   900   Knocktopher   13 New Ross

Clonmel 94   Inistioge 13

Ardfert 18   5   Charleville

Taghmon 13   900 Wexford

13 Tralee

Doneraile N/A   500   13 Clonmines

Dingle 163

N/A Mallow   Waterford   1000   13 Bannow

KERRY 1,000

Rathcormack 7   Tallow 96   50 Lismore   13 Fethard

C O R K 3,000

13 plus freeman

Castlemartyr 13   120 Dungarvan

Cork 1206   8   Youghal

Midleton

Bandon 75   Kinsale

13 plus freeman

5   Clonakilty

11   Baltimore

0   20 km

0   20 miles

N

effect, the Irish patriots now had their own volunteer army.

They duly achieved their goal in 1782 when the Irish parliament achieved its "independence" of Westminster. The statutes that had made Dublin subordinate legislatively were repealed and The Old House on College Green – as it was to be known in romance thereafter – entered into its brief pomp. It may have been free of Westminster, but it was not free of the Dublin Castle administration which for the most part had no truck with patriot sentiment and which still controlled the levers of administrative power. There was a never resolved tension between the two ends of Dame Street.

There was a further complication. When the Volunteers were founded it was ostensibly to protect Ireland in the absence of the army. But against what exactly was it protecting the country? The French, was an obvious and a correct answer. But there was also a nervous if undeclared need to protect the ascendancy against any resurgence from the dispossessed Catholic majority. The Volunteers may have been watching the coasts and watching for their chance with London, but they were also watching their backs.

None the less, there were liberal elements in the Volunteer/patriot movement who wished to lessen Catholic legal disabilities. Gardiner's relief acts of 1778 and 1782 represented the first formal easing of the Penal Laws. But there were also significant figures among the patriots who feared such liberal reforms. This difference of opinion was to prove significant in 1800, at the time of the Act of Union. And outside the ranks of the patriots, ascendancy figures more closely associated with the Castle administration – powerful figures like the attorney-general John Fitzgibbon, later lord chancellor under the title Lord Clare – were adamantine in their opposition to Catholic relief and nervous about any further weakening of the connection with England.

These factions were not just political in the larger sense. They also echoed some of the controversies concerning the ongoing development of the city of Dublin. Plans to continue the eastward development of the city were the cause of bitter public controversy. The building of the Custom House – now regarded as the finest single classical structure in the city – was especially so. The architect James Gandon was a protégé of John Beresford, the First Commissioner of Revenue and an important and influential figure in the Castle administration. In tandem with Luke Gardiner, Beresford developed the area of Lower Gardiner Street, Lower Abbey Street and Beresford Place as well as the Custom House itself.

Beresford's position in the Castle was enough to arouse patriot opposition to his plans, opposition which was echoed by merchant interests which did not want any further eastward drift of the city's commerce. The most prominent of the patriots, Henry Grattan, was a vociferous opponent of the new Custom

Opposite: Powerscourt House in South William Street.

House. So was James Napper Tandy, one of the founders of the United Irishmen. The city mob was mobilised in opposition, to the point where Gandon felt obliged to wear a sword when visiting the site. None the less, the work proceeded and by 1791, after ten years of heroic labour on a site which was all reclaimed slobland, the great Custom House was completed. It is impossible to think of modern Dublin without it.

There is little doubt that Gardiner and Beresford, each of them members of the Wide Streets Commission, abused their positions in order to profit from the development of lands which they owned. By any modern standards, their conduct was self-serving if not downright corrupt and one can more readily understand the otherwise incomprehensible opposition to the Custom House when one bears this in mind. Moreover, it was seen as Beresford's personal project, and Beresford was both high-handed and deeply unpopular. He has also been vindicated by the outcome, which may be insufficient justification for the squeamish but is its own reward.

Gandon was *the* architect of Dublin golden age. The only rival that the Custom House faces for the prize of greatest building in the city is his Four Courts, built farther upstream on the north bank of the river near the ancient Átha Cliath from which the city takes its Irish-language name. This monumental structure dominates the upper reaches of the river. The foundation stone was laid in 1786 and the building was finished in 1801, although it was sufficiently advanced by 1796 for the courts to use it.

He was also responsible for the brilliantly successful eastern addition to Lovett Pearce's Parliament House. This created a new entrance to the House of Lords with its portico and Corinthian columns projected over the street pavement. The pavement in question in 1789, when this work was completed, was that of Fleet Lane, a narrow thoroughfare that crossed Fleet Street and terminated at the river on Aston Quay.

Fleet Lane soon became Westmoreland Street. As part of the last major undertaking sponsored by the Wide Street Commissioners, the river was bridged at the end of Sackville Street when Carlisle Bridge was opened in 1795. Two new streets were built to complete the connection of the Gardiner and Beresford estates on the north side, centred on Sackville Street, to the Parliament House and Trinity. Westmoreland Street and D'Olier Street date from the early years of the nineteenth century, but their genesis lay in the closing years of the old century. They gave the city a new central north-south axis which it has never lost.

Gandon was also partly responsible for the design of the King's Inns at the head of Henrietta Street, the other architect being his pupil Henry Aaron Baker. It is a fine building but occupies a part of the city that was to suffer badly during the nineteenth-century decline and that has hardly felt any effect from the

so-called Celtic Tiger boom of the 1990s and 2000s. It stands as a distinguished orphan in an otherwise neglected and shabby urban environment.

This western end of the Gardiner estate was one of the more conspicuous areas where the energy gave out. Plans to build a royal circus at the western end of Eccles Street, where the Mater Hospital and Berkeley Street church now stand, were never realised. This early decline on the western fringe of the city was, in a sense, the mirror image of continuing developments to the east. The Merrion/Pembroke estate, in particular, continued to demonstrate its vitality in the development of Fitzwilliam Square, the last of the classical Dublin squares to be constructed. Begun in the 1790s, it was not completed until the 1820s. It is smaller and more intimate than its near neighbour, Merrion Square, or than Mountjoy Square on the north side. Its charm is largely a function of this smaller size.

On its eastern flank, the square is an extension of Upper Fitzwilliam Street which, together with Lower Fitzwilliam Street and Fitzwilliam Place, runs from the south-east corner of Merrion Square across the junction with Baggot Street and all the way up to Leeson Street. The entire vista thus created was over a kilometre long and – subject to a few footling variations of theme here and there – uniformly classical. It was by far the longest continuous Georgian streetscape in Dublin and one of the longest anywhere. It survived as such until the barbarism of the 1960s – that deadly decade for architecture – disturbed its uniformity.

Among the other buildings of classical Dublin that were neither developed by the great estates nor designed by James Gandon, the Royal Exchange deserves particular mention. With the development of Dame Street and the building of Parliament Street, the site at the junction of these streets acquired a strategic and visual importance it had previously lacked. This was the site chosen for a new Royal Exchange to replace the previous building in Winetavern Street. It was a meeting place for the traders and merchants of the city to transact business, operating on the same essential principle as a modern stock exchange.

The competition to design the new Royal Exchange was won by Thomas Cooley, a Londoner and one of the many architects busily engaged in the wholesale redevelopment of the nearby Castle and the creation of the Upper Castle Yard. Work began in 1769 and it took ten years to build. The result is magnificent, one of the very finest buildings in Dublin, doing justice to its sensitive position by enclosing the view along Capel Street, across the river and up Parliament Street. It ceased to discharge its original function in 1852 and has since served as the City Hall.

Classical Dublin was a city of contrasts, as is every city in every era. The

Grattan's Parliament,
1779–80.

superb streetscapes and noble public buildings were cheek-by-jowl with foetid slums and rank poverty. Ireland was still in many respects a marchland, a frontier land. Its aristocracy, according to Jonah Barrington's famous tripartite taxonomy, comprised Gentlemen to the Backbone, Gentlemen Every Inch of Them and Half-Mounted Gentlemen. Quite what the distinction was between the first two categories is obscure but there is no doubting the third. The hard-drinking, hard-gambling, roistering, duelling squireens were the Half-Mounted element. Their urban equivalents were the bucks and pinkindindies, and the wild young men in Daly's Club on College Green whose idea of amusement was to take pot shots at the statues in the grounds of St Andrew's church nearby. The roaring boys were as emblematic of the time as the cultivated gentlemen.

At the centre of the city's life stood parliament, the Old House on College Green. An Irish parliament had existed since the thirteenth century, for most of its existence limited and circumscribed in its powers. But since the winning of legislative independence in 1782, it was a real force in the land. The rising of the United Irishmen in 1798 shattered the complacent certainties of its world and of the ascendancy world generally. Panicked by an insurrection that seemed to combine a nightmare junction of Catholic peasant revival and French revolutionary principles, the ascendancy was persuaded and bribed to abolish its own parliament and effect a union with Great Britain. The two kingdoms would now be one, the United Kingdom. So it became on 1 January 1801. For Dublin, it was the end of the golden age.

Jonah

Jonah Barrington (1760–1834) was a cynical, calculating, worldly charmer. A barrister, he entered the Irish parliament in 1790 and was for the most part a government supporter. This support was given not entirely on grounds of principle – Barrington was too much fun for that – but in part on the calculation that the patriot opposition (Grattan *et al*) were superior in ability. He reckoned accordingly that he might shine more readily on the government side of the house.

He prospered both in parliament and at the Bar. He was a vociferous public opponent of the Act of Union, although he claimed to have been offered the post of solicitor-general to support it. However, he did allow himself to be used by the government to bribe others to support the Union. He was knighted and appointed to the bench, but – living as he did a florid financial life – he peculated funds lodged in his court and was eventually removed from the bench for these misappropriations. He spent the last twenty years of his life in Paris, the sensible man.

He was also a diarist of genius, unfailingly entertaining, self-serving and unreliable. In his *Personal Sketches and Recollections*, he has left us accounts of upper-class Dublin life in the 1790s that ring true, as here, describing events in a lodging house where he was staying as a young lawyer:

"One day, after dinner, Lord Mountnorris seemed less communicative than usual, but not less cheerful. He took out his watch, made a speech, as customary, drank his tipple, as he denominated the brandy and water, but seemed rather impatient. At length, a loud rap announced somebody of consequence, and the Marquis of Ely was named."

It transpired that Ely was acting as Mountnorris's second in a duel. Barrington and friends pursued his lordship. "Our pursuit exceeded a mile, when in the distance I perceived that the coach had stopped at Donnybrook-fair green, where, on every eighth of June, many an eye seems to mourn for the broken skull that had protected it from expulsion. I took my time, as I was now sure of my game, and had just reached the field when I heard the firing.

Gam and Kyle [his friends] had flown towards the spot, and nearly tumbled over my lord, who had received a bullet from the Hon. Francis Hely Hutchinson, late collector for Dublin, on the right side, directly under his lordship's pistol arm. The peer had staggered and measured his length on the green sward, and I certainly thought it was all over with him. I stood snugly all the while behind my tree, not wishing to have anything to do with the coroner's inquest, which I considered inevitable. To my astonishment, however, I saw my lord arise! And after some colloquy, the combatants bowed to each other and separated; my lord got back to his coach with aid and reached Frederick Street, if not in quite as good health, certainly with as high a character for bravery as when he had left it. Indeed, never did any person enjoy a wound more sincerely!"

Mountnorris survived. Duelling was ubiquitous among gentlemen in late eighteenth-century Ireland, albeit illegal – which explains Barrington's characteristic evasion in the matter of the prospective inquest. In what was still something of a frontier society, raw physical courage was valued as a virility test and the question "Does he blaze?" needed to be answered in the affirmative to establish macho credentials.

As for Barrington, he is the great unreliable narrator of his time, incapable of writing a dull sentence even if he tried. Not a good man, perhaps, but a good companion.

View of Merrion Square from Leinster Lawn, taken in the late nineteenth century.

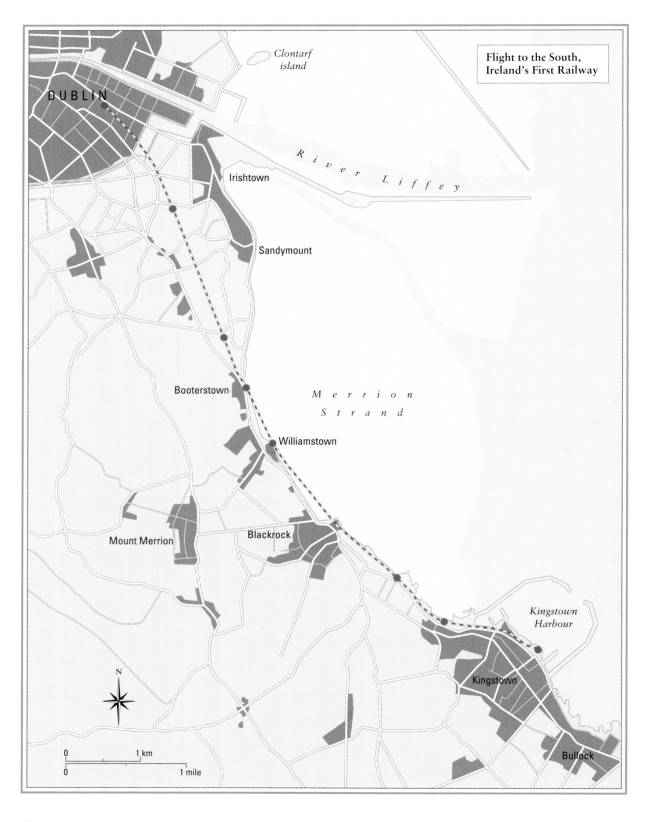

Clontarf island

DUBLIN

Flight to the South,
Ireland's First Railway

River Liffey

Irishtown

Sandymount

Merrion Strand

Booterstown

Williamstown

Mount Merrion

Blackrock

Kingstown Harbour

N

Kingstown

Bullock

0   1 km
0   1 mile

— CHAPTER 9 —
DECLINE

It is one of the great truisms of Dublin history to state that the city went into a steep decline after the Union. There is no arguing the point, although it will bear some qualification. The basic case is unanswerable. Once Dublin ceased to be a centre of independent – or at least autonomous – political power, ambition and style gravitated towards London. There was no longer any requirement to come to Dublin to attend parliament, so MPs, their servants, retainers and entourages found it easier to resettle in London, or to go there directly from their country estates, bypassing the capital.

This did not all happen at once, or in a rush. But it happened progressively over time. The effect was the gradual abandonment of many fine houses and their conversion to other purposes, not least – especially in the second half of the nineteenth century – to degraded tenement slums. This process was most marked in that north-western quadrant of the city that was the first to be abandoned by fashion. The canal basin at Broadstone – and later the railway station adjacent – brought commercial traffic into the heart of this area, further lowering its prestige. This process accounts for the distressed condition of Dominick Street by the late nineteenth century, when it was a conspicuous example of slum misery. Before the Union, it had been one of the noblest streets in the city.

The first railway journey in Ireland. As the initial service of the Dublin & Kingstown Railway leaves Westland Row Station and crossed Barrow Street bridge, 1834.

The decisive movement of fashion was from north-west to south-east. The Pembroke/Fitzwilliam estate, centred on Merrion and Fitzwilliam Squares and their surrounding streets, retained their insulation from the unpleasant world of commerce. Moreover, the first railway in Ireland opened in 1834 on the northern margins of this estate at Westland Row and provided a new commuter link to the shoreline of the southern bay, from which followed gradual suburban development and the possibility of flight from the less pleasant aspects of the city – not least its taxes – to charming seaside villas.

By skirting the edge of the Pembroke/Fitzwilliam estate, this railway – the Dublin & South-Eastern – gave access to and from fashionable Dublin without impinging on it physically. In this, it contrasts with the other three main Dublin rail termini, all of which had a disimproving effect on their immediate areas, or accelerated a decline already present. The Great Northern terminus at Amiens Street (now Connolly) was on the edge of the Gardiner estate, already declining in prestige as fashion fled south. The Great Southern & Western's magnificent station at Kingsbridge (now Heuston) was at the western end of the Liffey quays, in a traditionally poor area. Likewise, we have noted the effect of the Midland Great Western terminus at Broadstone. In general, railway stations did nothing for the social prestige of their surroundings, in Dublin or anywhere else.

The gradual flight of wealth from north to south, and also out of the city altogether, left a greater proportion the poor and impoverished behind, and emphasised with stark clarity just how desperate life at the bottom was. The best and earliest testimony we have comes from the reports of a heroic clergyman, Rev. James Whitelaw. As early as 1805, he produced a report based on his many visitations to the homes of the poor. The scenes he described and the causes to which he ascribed the wretched poverty and ill-health of the Dublin poor were to find echoes throughout the nineteenth century and beyond.

He described conditions of incredible overcrowding, with sometimes even single rooms being sub-divided to provide a minimal and miserable living space. He left graphic and disgusting accounts of the complete absence of any sanitary clearance system and the consequent concentration of dung heaps – for human and animal waste alike – and rubbish middens in enclosed back yards. One quotation from his 1805 report will suffice: "Into the back-yard of each house, frequently not ten feet deep, is flung from the windows of each apartment the ordure and filth of its numerous inhabitants; from whence that it is so seldom removed that I have seen it on a level with the windows of the first floor; and the moisture that, after heavy rain, oozes from the heap, having frequently no sewer to carry it off, runs into the street by the entry leading to the staircase."

Commercial activity such as brewing and soap manufacture also produced noxious or filthy by-products. There were lime-kilns in residential areas. There were open sewers everywhere in poor areas. People living in vastly overcrowded conditions and in close proximity to such ubiquitous filth were obviously prone to infectious diseases, the causes of which were still not properly understood or acknowledged. For example, there were devastating outbreaks of cholera in 1818 and 1832.

In addition, the city was still small, almost wholly contained within the two canals. In this limited space, the population had risen to more than 200,000 people. Even with growing social segregation, wealth and poverty were uncomfortably close. Wealth demanded servants, and servants could carry infec-

Dublin seen looking east from Phoenix Park.

tious diseases from the slums to the homes of the mighty. Professions such as doctors and clergymen were especially vulnerable. Moreover, social segregation was incomplete. Even the wealthiest parts of the city had slums adjacent. The area immediately north of Merrion Square was one such, which is why it was all right for the Dublin & South-Eastern Railway to punch through the slums to its terminus at Westland Row. The area remains a poor one to this day.

The south-west of the city, immediately outside the ancient city walls, was the poorest of all. Known as the Liberties – from the medieval liberties of St Sepulchre, the Earl of Meath, and others – it was the one area that had been largely untouched by eighteenth-century splendour. It was here that Whitelaw found the very worst conditions. In 1818, he recorded that in the Liberties there were "many large houses, consisting of a number of rooms; each of these rooms is let to separate tenants, who again re-let them to as many individuals as they can contain, each person paying for that portion of the floor which his extended body can occupy".

It was out of this impoverished quarter that there emerged one of the city's tragic romances. Robert Emmet had been well born, the son of the state physician. He was educated at Trinity, from which he was expelled in 1798 – that climactic year – in a purge of radical undergraduates. He had joined the United Irishmen and when their rebellion (in which he played no part) failed, he maintained contact with some of the survivors. Following in the footsteps

Opposite: *A stylised image of Robert Emmet at his trial.*

of Wolfe Tone, he went to France to solicit military aid from Napoleon for a further attempt. None was forthcoming and by the autumn of 1802 he was back in Ireland.

He hatched an elaborate plan to stage a coup d'etat in Dublin once England was once more at war with France, which it was from early 1803. The plan entailed a raid for arms on the Pigeon House garrison at Ringsend which, when successful, would be announced by the firing of a rocket into the sky. This would be the signal for other bodies of rebels to rise. Emmet greatly exaggerated the number of potential supporters at his disposal, by including numbers of the city's poor in his calculations. This caused some of the other potential leaders, including Michael Dwyer of Wicklow, a veteran of '98, to suspect Emmet's fitness for the role he had assumed. Dwyer was a dedicated revolutionary, and he had a distrust of potentially undisciplined mobs which would have not been amiss in the mouth of a regular army officer. His doubts about attracting a *canaille* in support of a rebellion were to be justified by events.

None of Emmet's elaborate plans materialised. Worse, an arms depot in Patrick Street exploded on 16 July 1803, threatening to unravel and reveal the entire conspiracy. This led Emmet to bring forward the date of the rising to 23 July and to focus only on an attempt to capture Dublin Castle. It was a fiasco. Emmet marched a group of eighty or so men, many of them the worse for drink, through the Liberties to Thomas Street, there to muster for an assault on the Castle. Dressed in a dashing green military jacket and a plumed hat he tried to enthuse the local populace, which declined to be enthused. Realising the hopelessness of his situation, he abandoned the attempt on the Castle and fled south, towards Wicklow. Unfortunately, his men now turned into a leaderless mob and for about two hours they held Thomas Street and James's Street in what was effectively a riotous assembly.

By the time order was restored by troops from the Castle, about fifty people were killed including the notably liberal Lord Kilwarden, the chief justice, and his nephew. They were piked to death by the mob. By a bitter irony, Kilwarden's family name was Wolfe: they were a landed family from Co. Kildare. In 1763, the head of the family had been one Theobald Wolfe, in whose honour one of his tenants, Peter Tone, a coachman, had named his eldest son.

Emmet's myth proceeds from the nature of his capture and death. He was in love with Sarah Curran, the daughter of John Philpott Curran, the most famous Irish barrister of the day and a man who had been personally close to the United men in 1798. Whether Sarah Curran requited Emmet's obvious devotion to her is uncertain, but his eventual capture by the authorities was due to his refusing safe passage to France until he could see her. Songs and ballads were written in memory of this doomed love affair, the best known of them

Thomas Moore's "She Is Far From the Land".

Emmet then ensured his immortality in the Irish tradition by his speech from the dock following his inevitable conviction for high treason. It is one of the most famous speeches in Irish history. Unfortunately, there is no definitive text of the speech, for it was delivered extempore and without notes or a draft (or at least any that has survived). The standard version now used probably includes embellishments added posthumously by nationalist enthusiasts. None the less, the substance of the speech as we know it was that delivered by Emmet and as recorded by a distinguished court reporter present and by others. Most disputes turn on the famous peroration which may indeed be a later nationalist invention. Equally, however, it was in keeping with a notably eloquent and courageous address and it may simply have been bowdlerised by the Castle. Whichever is the case, the standard version now accepted is a stirring oration, one of the greatest ever delivered in the city.

Emmet was hanged and beheaded in Thomas Street on 20 September and his body buried at Bully's Acre in the grounds of the Royal Hospital, Kilmainham. He was just twenty-five when he died.

The early years of the nineteenth century did not see the city simply collapse into a slough of poverty, rebellion and neglect. The Royal College of Surgeons in Ireland opened its splendid new building on the west side of St Stephen's Green in 1806, thus giving the least fashionable side of the Green a building of distinction. In Sackville Street, the Dublin architect *du jour*, Francis Johnston, built a new General Post Office (1814–18) which dominates the street to this day. Ironically, both the GPO and the College of Surgeons were to play key roles in the events of 1916 in which the spirit of Robert Emmet was so often invoked. Johnston was also principally responsible for Nelson Pillar (1808), the city's icon for more than a century and a half. It was built to commemorate the British victory at Trafalgar three years earlier, which gave the Royal Navy control of the seas for a hundred years. The Pillar was blown up in 1966 by persons also inclined to invoke Emmet's ghost.

Another city icon, the Ha'penny Bridge, dates from 1816. It is formally known as Wellington Bridge, in memory of the victor of Waterloo the previous year, himself one of the city's more reluctant sons. It is also sometimes referred to as the Metal Bridge, and with some justice, because it is one of the earliest examples in Ireland of a single-span metal bridge. However, its most famous moniker refers to the toll of one halfpenny that was levied to cross it (it was and is purely a pedestrian bridge) from its opening until 1919. In 1820, a more substantial memorial to the Iron Duke was completed in the form of the Wellington Monument in the Phoenix Park, the biggest obelisk in Europe. It was built in three years, but did not assume its final appearance until the bronze panels commemorating Wellington's victories were put in place in 1861. They were cast from cannon captured in the Peninsular War.

In an earlier chapter, we noted the building of the Bull Wall on the north of the bay. This work was completed in 1820, the year that the long reign of King George III ended. He was succeeded by the former Prince Regent, now George IV, a dissipated sot. The new king visited Dublin 1821, the first English king ever to visit Ireland for a wholly peaceful purpose. He arrived drunk.

The original intention had been to land at the new mail packet harbour of Dunleary, which was to be renamed Kingstown in his honour. However, he was so far gone in drink that it was felt that the waiting crowd would be scandalised by the sight of their sovereign in a distressed condition. He was taken across the bay to the fishing port of Howth and put ashore there. The point at the end of the west pier where he first trod on Irish soil is commemorated by an impressed set of his footprints, still present there.

The king's visit was a great success, albeit the man was racked by diarrhoea. He went to the Curragh races where a vast travelling commode was provided for his sole use and was pressed into frequent and regular service. His Majesty departed as he had meant to come, through Kingstown as it was now to be called for a century. His was the first of series of occasional royal visits in the course of the nineteenth and early twentieth centuries: Queen Victoria, Edward VII and George V all visited the city. Indeed, Edward had good reason to remember Ireland with affection: while still Prince of Wales and serving with the army at the Curragh in 1861, he had his first sexual experience. His partner, introduced to his bed by his fellow-officers, was a local "actress", one Nellie Clifton. She deserves her footnote in history, for she initiated a career of heroic philandering on the part of the prince. News of this event reached the ears of his father, Prince Albert, and apparently hastened that poor man's decline.

In general, the first half of the nineteenth century is not regarded as one of the city's great eras. The shadow of the classical age lay too heavily across it. None the less, there were developments that were decisive for the future and significant in themselves. The opening of the Pro-Cathedral in 1825 was a public statement that the penal era was long in the past. While the established church still held the ancient cathedrals of Christ Church and St Patrick's and the new Catholic cathedral was obliged to locate itself discreetly in a quiet quarter parallel to Sackville Street, its official consecration was a seminal moment. Four years later, Daniel O'Connell secured the passage of the Catholic Emancipation Act at Westminster, removing nearly all residual legal disabilities against Catholics. There followed an explosion of Catholic church building during the rest of the century, as well as the development and expansion of Catholic schools, teaching orders and hospitals. Dublin had ceased to be a

Protestant city. Its Catholic majority was about to make its political voice heard.

In 1830, there was founded one of the city's most enduring and best-loved amenities, the Zoo. Situated then as now in the Phoenix Park, it is the second-oldest zoological gardens in the British Isles after Regent's Park in London. A less loved institution was formed in 1836 with the introduction of a new police service along the lines pioneered by the London Metropolitan Police (1829). The Irish Constabulary was formed as an armed gendarmerie for the country outside Dublin. The capital got its own unarmed force, the Dublin Metropolitan Police (DMP) at the same time, thus putting urban policing on a recognisably modern footing.

We have already noted the foundation of the Irish railway system, radiating from a Dublin hub, in 1834, and facilitating the development of the southern seaside suburbs. The spread of the railway system drew middle-class people away from the decaying city centre in the course of the century, resulting in the creation of a series of nine independent townships where local taxation was lighter than in the city. This was a serious development, for the city could ill-afford the erosion of its revenue base given the scale of the social and economic problems it faced. In effect, the flight to the townships was the new middle class giving up on the city itself. The independent townships survived until 1930 when they were reincorporated into the metropolitan area.

City government did take a major step forward in 1840 as a result of the Municipal Corporations (Ireland) Act of that year. The net effect was to make city government more representative and less oligarchic. In place of the old series of nominating bodies, all of them exclusively Protestant, the Corporation was now elected by all rate-paying property owners. The measure had been part of a deal made between the Whig government in London and Daniel O'Connell, the hero of the Catholic Emancipation struggle and the champion of Irish nationalism. As a result of this measure, O'Connell became lord mayor of the city in the following year, the first Catholic to hold the office since 1688.

Daniel O'Connell in the robes of the Lord Mayor of Dublin.

Opposite: *The Zoo, in Phoenix Park, a favourite with generations of Dubliners.*

Pillar

On 15 February 1808, the duke of Richmond, lord lieutenant of Ireland, laid the foundation stone in the centre of Sackville Street for a pillar to commemorate Horatio Nelson, whose victory over the Franco-Spanish fleet at Trafalgar three years earlier gave Britain a command of the seas as decisive as Napoleon had secured on land at the Battle of Austerlitz in the same year.

The principal architect of Nelson Pillar was Francis Johnston, who had succeeded Gandon as the leader of his profession in Dublin. Johnston was also responsible for the General Post Office, just beside the Pillar and the dominant building in the street. He designed the Pillar as a single Doric column of Wicklow granite, rising 134 feet from the base and topped by a statue of Nelson.

The Pillar established itself as the spiritual centre of the city, the terminus point for trams and busses, a meeting place for assignations of every sort. It also offered a panoramic view of the city centre if you were content to slog up the spiral steps to the viewing platform beside the statue. In *Ulysses*, Stephen invents a story to amuse his companions concerning two old Dublin women – Anne Kearns and Florence MacCabe – who climb the Pillar and consume a bag of plums which they have bought, spitting the plum stones out through the railings to fall on the crowds below. They were not alone in that pursuit.

The physical impact of the Pillar is best seen in nineteenth-century paintings by Michaelangelo Hayes (1850) and Charles Russell (1875). Its central position and vertical drama contrast with the long rectilinear horizontal of the street itself, broken only slightly by the projecting portico of the GPO. The classical unity of the original Georgian street was progressively subverted in the nineteenth century and a new order created, of which the Pillar was an organic part.

Yet Dublin was never quite sure about Nelson Pillar. It was frequently objected to on the grounds that it impeded the free flow of traffic. There was some truth in this, but the same could be said for any of the other statues and monuments in the street, which the Victorians erected with gusto. Indeed, the Parnell monument, at the north end of the street, was (and is) much more of a nuisance in this regard.

The real objection to the Pillar was political. In an ever more nationalist age, it seemed dissonant – to put it no stronger – to have a British imperial hero aloft on the most prominent monument in the Irish capital. From time to time, there were proposals floated to remove Nelson and replace him with a more appropriate figure. After the 1916 rising, Patrick Pearse was a name frequently mentioned. There were others mooted, both sacred and profane.

The matter was settled in the most decisive fashion in the early hours of 7 March 1966 by an IRA splinter group which wished to make its own contribution to the golden anniversary celebrations of the Easter rising. They blew up the Pillar, leaving only the stump. Miraculously, nobody was killed and the general consensus was that they had done a very neat job. Just how neat was underlined when the regular Irish army came to dispose of the stump, which they did but at the price of blowing out just about every window in the street.

Where once stood the Pillar, there now stands the Spire. Designed by the English architect Ian Ritchie, it stands three times the height of the old Pillar. It has no political or historical associations, being perfectly abstract. Like the Pillar, it seems to divide opinion, drawing praise and scorn in equal measure.

Painting by Charles Russell made in 1875 on the occasion of a rally to mark the centenary of Daniel O'Connell's birth. It shows the old Carlisle Bridge in the foreground before it was widened to its present extent, with Nelson Pillar prominent in the middle of Sackville Street.

Ireland's Railways
By 1900

CHAPTER 10
VICTORIANS

The reform of municipal government meant the consolidation of power in Dublin Corporation. Regulatory functions which had previously been chaotically dispersed among individual parishes and voluntary bodies were now subject to greater central control. The most impressive results were seen in areas like sanitation and public health, where the second half of the century brought major advances. The first medical health officer for the city was appointed in 1864 and a huge step forward took place with the opening of the Vartry waterworks in 1863. For the first time, it provided the city with a pure water supply at high pressure and was the envy of other, richer cities in Britain and abroad.

The chief promoter of this initiative was the chairman of the waterworks committee, Sir John Gray, whose statue stands in O'Connell Street. The Vartry's retaining dam held 11 million cubic metres, which then flowed through a 4km long tunnel to a large open service reservoir at Stillorgan before delivering up to 85,000 cubic metres daily to the city. Joyce rhapsodised the scheme in a bravura passage in *Ulysses*, set in the hot summer of 1904:

"From Roundwood reservoir in county Wicklow of a cubic capacity of 2400 million gallons, percolating through a subterranean aqueduct of filter mains of single and double pipeage constructed at an initial plant cost of 5 pounds per linear yard by way of the Dargle, Rathdown, Glen of the Downs and Callowhill to the 26 acre reservoir at Stillorgan, a distance of 22 statute miles, and thence, through a system of relieving tanks, by a gradient of 250 feet to the city boundary at Eustace bridge, upper Leeson street, though from prolonged summer drouth and daily supply of 12 1/2 million gallons the water had fallen below the sill of the overflow weir for which reason the borough surveyor and waterworks engineer, Mr Spencer Harty, C.E., on the instructions of the waterworks committee had prohibited the use of municipal water for purposes other than those of consumption (envisaging the possibility of recourse being had to the impotable water of the Grand and Royal canals as in 1893) particularly as the South Dublin Guardians, notwithstanding their ration of 15 gallons per day per pauper supplied through a 6 inch meter, had been convicted of a wastage of 20,000 gallons per night by a reading of their meter on the affirmation of the law agent of the corporation, Mr Ignatius Rice, solicitor, thereby acting to the detriment of another section of the public, self-supporting taxpayers, solvent, sound."

Hand in hand with this major advance in the city's infrastructure went the development of domestic plumbing and the city's sewer system. A Royal Commission on the Sewerage and Drainage of Dublin reported in 1880. It built on a sewerage system that had been begun in 1870 and was to develop into the Main Drainage Scheme in 1892, not reaching its full extent until 1906.

These developments were all the more urgent because of the growing population of the city, which was especially marked in the years following the catastrophic Great Famine of 1845–52. The city swelled with wretchedly poor people fleeing from the stricken countryside. This in turn accelerated the flight of the middle classes to the nine new townships: Rathmines & Rathgar, Pembroke, Blackrock, Kingstown, Dalkey, Killiney, Kilmainham, Drumcondra and Clontarf: all safely outside the ring of the two canals and therefore beyond the reach of the Corporation, each with its own local authority and town hall and with lower rates than the city.

The division of the classes is the big theme of Victorian Dublin. The poor remained in a decaying, hideously overcrowded centre, many living in conditions of squalor without parallel in northern Europe. The moneyed middle classes – ever more the social leaders of the city now that the flight of the old aristocracy was almost complete – lived in the townships, but worked, shopped and enjoyed concerts and theatres in the city to which they otherwise made no

This image, from a photograph dated as late as 1953, gives a vivid impression of the wretchedness of Dublin's tenement life.

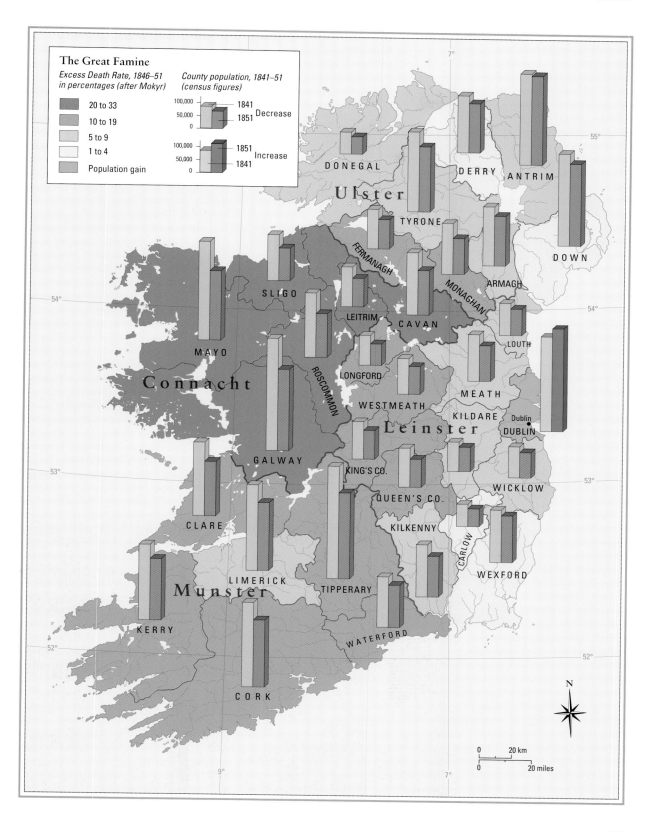

The Great Famine

Excess Death Rate, 1846–51
in percentages (after Mokyr)

20 to 33
10 to 19
5 to 9
1 to 4
Population gain

County population, 1841–51
(census figures)

100,000
50,000
0

1841
1851 Decrease

100,000
50,000
0

1851
1841 Increase

material contribution. As the city housing situation, especially in the tenements, went from bad to worse, with no clear plan for wholesale slum clearance, the suburbs witnessed a dramatic expansion with the development of delightful red-brick areas like Ranelagh, Ballsbridge, Blackrock and Kingstown. Later the north side followed suit with Drumcondra and Clontarf. Some of these had been outlying villages that were now swallowed up by the new developments, but the overall effect of this expansion was the creation of a stark binary class division. The continuing decay of the city and the development of lush suburbs were two sides of the one coin.

Dublin has as much claim to be a Victorian as a Georgian city, although the prestige of the Georgian architectural style was such that it persisted in the inner suburbs until about 1860. Not until after that does the assertively red-brick Victorian style come to dominate. As noted earlier, the suburbs hardly existed in 1800 and the entire population was contained within the canals. The suburban population was barely 30,000 in 1831. By 1891, the city population was just over 245,000 but that of the suburbs outside the Corporation area was already past 100,000. Those who could get out of town, got out.

Having got out, of course, they needed to get back in for work and pleasure. In this regard, the development of the tramway system was crucial. The first commercial tram ran in Dublin in 1872, on a route from the city to Rathmines. The tramway system spread rapidly, soon overwhelming the primitive omnibus network that had preceded it. In 1891, the three existing companies were consolidated as the Dublin United Tramway Company and the DUTC ran the city's first electric tram in 1896. The DUTC survived until 1945, bequeathing its much-loved "flying snail" logo to its unloved successor CIE.

Complementing access to and from the suburbs was the suburban railway system. Lines operated by the principal mainline companies were gradually studded with suburban halts to serve commuters' needs. The series of southside stations along the Dublin & South-Eastern line to Wexford still form the backbone of the modern Dublin Area Rapid Transit (DART) service. For example, Sydney Parade in the heart of the Pembroke township was opened as a station in 1852, having previously been a halt.

On the north side, the old Clontarf station on the GNR line to Belfast (not to be confused with the present DART station at Clontarf Road) opened in 1844. The suburb of Clontarf hardly existed in any coherent sense before this date: there were villages at the Sheds (at the end of the modern Vernon Avenue) and along the line of the Howth Road at Killester, but no concentrated development in between. Yet the foundation dates of churches and sports clubs gives a clue as to the arrival of a critical mass of people: the parish church of St John (CofI) dates from 1866, the Presbyterian church from 1890, the yacht club from

1875, the cricket and rugby clubs from 1876. A sprawling rural Catholic parish was subdivided into tighter suburban units between 1879 and 1909, as population numbers grew.

Clontarf can stand for all the other townships. The last third of the nineteenth century was the decisive period of suburban expansion, facilitated by the transport revolution. An early observer of the system noted the preponderance of bourgeois passengers on the trams. Maurice Brooks MP, the proprietor of one of the city's longest established building supply businesses, commented in 1879 that "the Dublin Tram Company has turned out very remunerative and in some respects a very useful institution, excellent returns to its proprietors, and proving of great convenience to passengers of the genteel and well-to-do class". He added that the company had "failed to confer equal advantages on the working or labouring class" by reason of its scheduling times and high fares.

The period from the 1850s to the mid 1870s was the high noon of Victorian prosperity in Britain. In Ireland outside east Ulster, it was the generation of recovery from the trauma of the Great Famine. Yet some of the optimism of the bigger island rubbed off on Dublin. In 1853, a major industrial exhibition was held in the city, on the lawns of the Royal Dublin Society, the sponsoring institution, at Leinster House facing onto Merrion Square. It was opened by Queen Victoria and Prince Albert and was an echo of London's Great Exhibition of 1851 in the

Classic Victorian red brick in the southside suburbs of Dublin. This was the prevailing style from 1860 until the Great War.

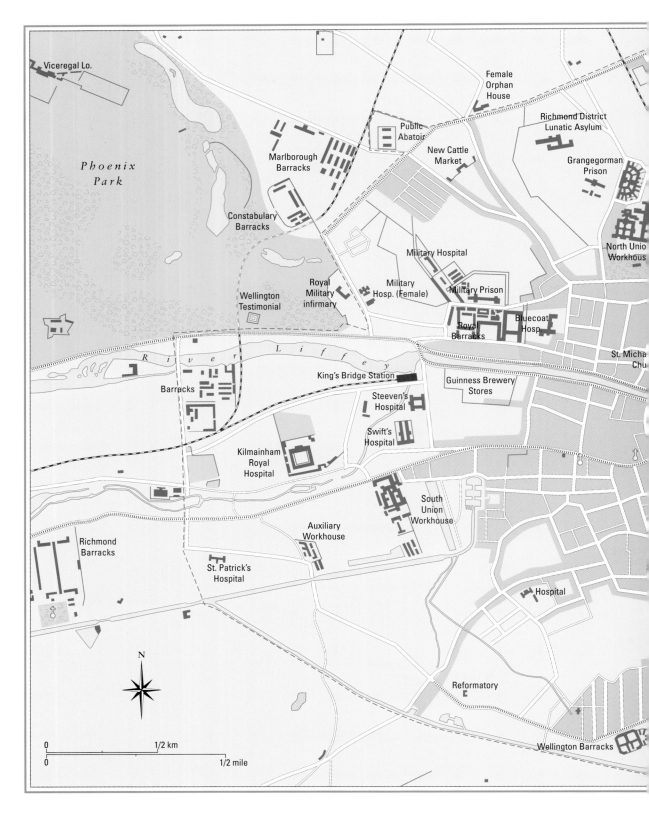

Viceregal Lo.

Phoenix Park

Marlborough Barracks

Constabulary Barracks

Public Abatoir

Female Orphan House

Richmond District Lunatic Asylum

New Cattle Market

Grangegorman Prison

Military Hospital

North Unio Workhous

Wellington Testimonial

Royal Military infirmary

Military Hosp. (Female)

Military Prison

Military Hosp. (Female)

Bluecoat Hosp.

Royal Barracks

River Liffey

King's Bridge Station

Guinness Brewery Stores

St. Micha Chu

Barracks

Steeven's Hospital

Swift's Hospital

Kilmainham Royal Hospital

South Union Workhouse

Auxiliary Workhouse

Richmond Barracks

St. Patrick's Hospital

Hospital

N

Reformatory

0   1/2 km

0   1/2 mile

Wellington Barracks

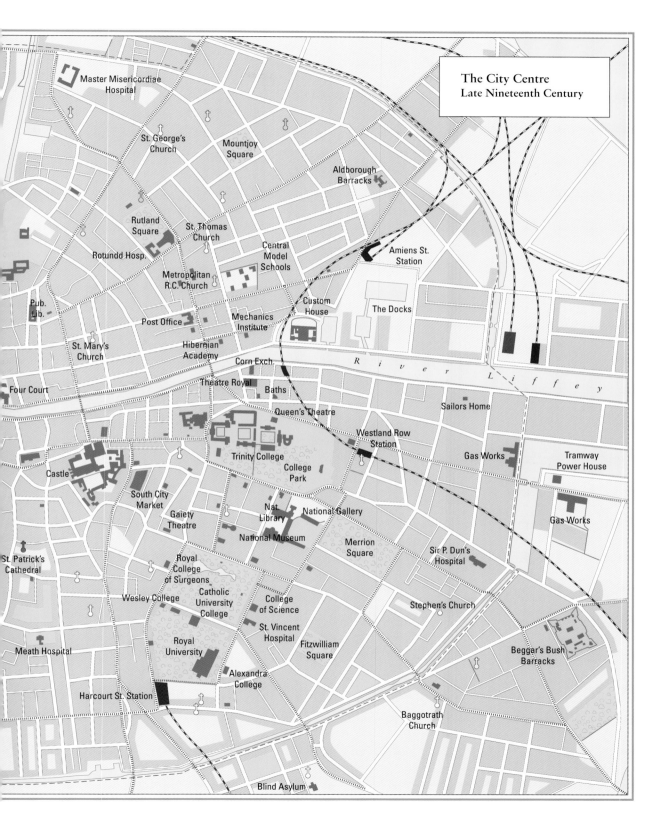

The City Centre
Late Nineteenth Century

Master Misericordiae Hospital

St. George's Church

Mountjoy Square

Aldborough Barracks

Rutland Square

St. Thomas Church

Central Model Schools

Amiens St. Station

Rotundd Hosp.

Metropolitan R.C. Church

Pub. Lib.

Post Office

Custom House

The Docks

St. Mary's Church

Mechanics Institute

Hibernian Academy

Corn Exch.

Four Court

Theatre Royal

Baths

River Liffey

Queen's Theatre

Sailors Home

Westland Row Station

Gas Works

Tramway Power House

Castle

Trinity College

College Park

South City Market

Gaiety Theatre

Nat. Library

National Gallery

Gas Works

National Museum

Merrion Square

Sir P. Dun's Hospital

St. Patrick's Cathedral

Royal College of Surgeons

Catholic University College

College of Science

Stephen's Church

Wesley College

St. Vincent Hospital

Fitzwilliam Square

Meath Hospital

Royal University

Beggar's Bush Barracks

Alexandra College

Harcourt St. Station

Baggotrath Church

Blind Asylum

Crystal Palace. A contemporary engraving of the opening ceremony shows a structure which looks a mimic of the Crystal Palace: the Dublin structure was in fact timber framed. The products of industry were a novelty in the 1850s – the industrial revolution was still in its early days and still almost unique to Britain – and the Dublin exhibition was partly intended for display and partly mounted in the hope of accelerating the post-Famine recovery. Given the absence of an industrial base outside Ulster, this well-meaning gesture proved futile.

The following year brought a significant if little noticed development. The Catholic University was founded with Cardinal Newman as its first rector. It is the lineal antecedent of UCD, now the largest institution of higher learning in Ireland. It started life in 86 St Stephen's Green, formerly the home of Bishop "Burnchapel" Whaley and his son, the famous Buck. Old Whaley might have turned in his grave when his house was renamed for Newman, who was not just a Catholic but a convert – an apostate. Right beside it, Newman commissioned a college chapel and got a gem. John Hungerford Pollen's University Church is a mock-Byzantine reproach to Protestant ecclesiastical austerity, its exuberant ornamentation and mosaics an assertion of architectural values that mirror the liturgical theatricality of Catholicism.

The appointment of Paul Cullen as Catholic Archbishop of Dublin in 1852 brought the most formidable cleric in nineteenth-century Ireland to the capital. An uncompromising Counter-Reformation Catholic, he had spent over twenty years as an influential figure in the Vatican before returning to Ireland. He was fearless, intelligent and formidable. He did little to soften sectarian tensions but he oversaw a huge institutional expansion of the church in the archdiocese during his twenty-six years in office. He encouraged the great expansion of Catholic education, a feature of the city's life throughout the century. Of the major Catholic schools, Belvedere dates from 1832, O'Connell's from the same decade. Synge Street CBS was founded in 1864. The Catholic presence in the professions was most marked in medicine, with UCD's medical school at Cecilia Street in Temple Bar establishing an early reputation. The opening of the Mater Hospital (1861) at the top of Eccles Street on the fringes of the old Gardiner estate was a major event in the city's history. Rome rewarded Cullen in 1866 by making him the first Irish cardinal.

Although he had no liking for British rule in Ireland, Cullen had even less time for nationalist secret societies, which explained his inveterate hatred for the Fenians, whose abortive rebellion of 1867 – it was scarcely less farcical than Emmet's effort – he denounced. One of the Fenians, John O'Leary, later told W.B. Yeats that in Ireland a man must either have the Church or the Fenians on his side, a lesson that Cullen understood instinctively and Parnell was to learn the hard way in 1891.

The same year that Newman founded his university brought an end of a very old tradition: Donnybrook Fair. The medieval village of Donnybrook, long distant from the city, was by the 1850s firmly in the path of the southward expansion of the Pembroke township. Indeed, the changing architectural style in domestic architecture, touched on earlier, is very obvious in the development of Donnybrook. The city end, nearest to Upper Leeson Street, is still built in a form of pared-down Georgian but by the time one advances down More-hampton Road towards the village, the style becomes unmistakeably Victorian suburban. At any rate, the new residents had not fled the city to endure the riot of Donnybrook Fair. They bought out the original charter that was the legal sanction for the event, which was thereby suppressed.

This replacement of ancient riot by modernising order was at least as emblematic of the age as the continued chaos in the city's housing situation. As symbols of that order, the opening of the National Gallery of Ireland in 1864 and of the National Library and National Museum in 1890 represent key moments in furnishing Dublin with a civic infrastructure. The Gallery was the product of the philanthropy of William Dargan, the railway engineer, who had bankrolled the 1853 exhibition and was reputed to have lost £20,000 in the process. The exhibition had included paintings, and the idea that there should be a city gallery took

The complex based on Leinster House. In the foreground, the National Museum. The National Library flanks Leinster House on the other side, with the National Gallery to the rear facing onto Merrion Square.

hold. The initial costs were met by public subscription and Dargan's seminal role was recalled by placing his statue outside the new building.

The Library and Museum were both products of legislation passed by parliament in 1877. In both instances, their core deposits were based on the holdings of the RDS and were specially donated for the purpose. The twin institutions occupied the wings of Leinster House, then the headquarters of the RDS. Another example of public-spirited philanthropy was the opening of the nearby St Stephen's Green as a public park in 1880. It had been the private domain of the Lords Iveagh, heirs to the Guinness fortune, prior to that.

In 1882, the Phoenix Park Murders shocked the city and the country and made international headlines. A group calling themselves the Invincibles, a Fenian offshoot, butchered the new chief secretary, Lord Frederick Cavendish and the under-secretary, Thomas Burke, within sight of the Viceregal Lodge. Cavendish was a nephew of Gladstone and had just arrived in Dublin to take up his appointment. Burke – the real target of the assassins – was the head of the Dublin Castle administration. The long-term repercussions of this horrible crime included an attempt by *The Times* to implicate Charles Stewart Parnell, the unquestioned leader of Irish nationalism, by printing forged letters suggesting he had foreknowledge of the plot. The charge did not stand up to scrutiny and Parnell's vindication left his stock at an all-time high: he had persuaded Gladstone to introduce a home rule bill for Ireland in 1886 which would have restored the domestic autonomy of an Irish parliament. Although the measure was lost in Westminster, it seemed only a matter of time before it would succeed. Parnell's fall from grace in 1890-91 was all the greater for the height to which he had previously ascended. Dublin remained a Parnell stronghold to the end, and his funeral in October 1891 was one of the biggest and most moving the city has ever seen.

The years after the fall of Parnell are conventionally thought of as those in which culture displaced politics in nationalist Ireland. Certainly, the country and the city displayed a revived cultural vitality. The founding of the Gaelic League in 1893 influenced the new generation of nationalists in a manner hitherto unthinkable, stressing the importance of native custom and language. Cross-pollinated with politics in the revolutionary era to come, it made for a heady brew.

The founding of the Irish Literary Theatre in 1899 was followed five years later by the Abbey, giving Ireland what is usually said to be its national theatre. But while its general purpose served nationalism, it did not scruple to subvert nationalist shibboleths. Unlike the Gaelic League which, although founded by the Protestant Douglas Hyde, was overwhelmingly Catholic in membership, the Abbey was a curious hybrid of Anglo-Irish mavericks and the nationalist

mainstream, with the former in control. Yeats and Lady Gregory were the moving spirits and J.M. Synge the playwright of genius who made the theatre's reputation. In the process, he so offended nationalist piety in *The Playboy of the Western World* that the play sparked a famous riot, not entirely to Yeats' chagrin – for the poet was a bonny fighter and welcomed a chance to rebuke the canaille de haut en bas.

The second half of the nineteenth saw a restructuring and expansion of Dublin port, that critical artery in the city's economic life. Its governance was vested in a new Port & Docks Board in 1868. The opening of Alexandra Basin in 1885 added to the port's capacity and gave it a deep-water berthage that it previously lacked. A new swivel bridge was built just west of the Custom House in 1879 and named for the patriot Isaac But. It survived in that form, which allowed shipping to pass through it, until 1932 when the present solid structure replaced it. Right beside it, in 1891, was erected one of the city's true eyesores, the Loop Line bridge, built to connect Westland Row and Amiens Street railway stations. More happily, Carlisle/O'Connell Bridge was widened in 1880 to the same width as Lower Sackville Street, leaving it literally as long as it is broad, one of the few truly square bridges in the world.

In the port itself, rail connections were eventually, after much delay, provided by the MGW and GSW companies to train sheds along the North Wall. The latter of these, known colloquially as the Southern Point, stood at the junction of the North Wall and East Wall Road. It was taken out of service as a goods terminal in the 1970s and converted as a concert venue, the Point, in the 1980s, undergoing a further transformation as the O_2 concert venue in recent years. The basic superstructure of the old Southern Point shed is still there, now topped by an incongruous and undistinguished architectural hat.

Any discussion of the port brings us back to the men who worked there and to the conditions in which they lived. The conditions were for the most part wretched and exploitative, with casual unskilled labour predominating. It left men with very little to offer the labour market other than their broad backs, leaving them largely at the mercy of employers. Into this unequal world there now irrupted one of the great forces of nature in the city's history, Jim Larkin.

He had been born in Liverpool and left school at eleven to work on the docks. In 1907, at the age of 31, he came to Ireland to organise the Belfast branch of the National Union of Dock Labourers. By August of that year he was in Dublin organising the NUDL there. He mobilised the casual dockers and within the year had tripped off three strikes, much to the chagrin of the NUDL head office in Britain which refused to finance them. Larkin was never an easy colleague. Disgusted with the NUDL, he proceeded to form his own union, the Irish Transport & General Workers (IT&GWU) in 1909. Over the next few years, his increasing militancy made him the sworn enemy of the Dublin employers. The climactic moment came in 1913, when William Martin Murphy, the dominant personality among the employers and proprietor of the Dublin United Tramway Company, locked out members of the IT&GWU who refused to sign a pledge to leave the union.

It was personal. Murphy and Larkin – each a big ego – detested each other. In response to the lockout, Larkin called a general strike at the end of August. Five days later, a heavily disguised Larkin entered the Imperial Hotel in Sackville Street, which was owned by Murphy, and began to harangue the crowd from a first-floor window. It was a audacious *coup de theatre*. The DMP over-reacted to the excited crowd, whom they baton charged: over 300 members of the public were injured. "Bloody Sunday" gave Larkin a moral victory. But the material victory eventually lay with the implacable Murphy. By early 1914, the men were effectively starved back to work. Every hand was against Larkin: the employers, naturally; the Catholic church, for the most part, ever suspicious of socialists; the mainstream nationalists, good bourgeois to a man; the British trades unions, who showed a most unfraternal attitude towards Larkin the longer the dispute went on.

Murphy and the employers had won, but historically it was a Pyrrhic victory. The poor of Dublin, living in conditions almost without parallel in the developed world, had a cause. Even if it was a losing cause for now, it was the making of a myth and labour relations in the city were never the same again. The writer and painter George Russell (AE) put it perfectly in his brilliant philippic, "An Address to the Masters of Dublin", in *The Irish Times* in October 1913:

"You do not seem to read history, so as to learn its lessons. That you are an uncultivated class was obvious from recent utterances of some of you upon art. That you are incompetent men in the sphere in which you arrogate imperial powers is certain, because for many years, long before the present uprising of labour, your enterprises have been dwindling in the regard of investors, and this while you have carried them on in the cheapest labour market in these islands, with a labour reserve always hungry and ready to accept any pittance. You are bad citizens, for we rarely, if ever, hear of the wealthy among you endowing your city with munificent gifts, which it is the pride of merchant princes in other cities to offer, and Irishmen not of your city who offer to supply the wants left by your lack of generosity are met with derision and abuse. Those who have economic power have civic power also, yet you have not used the power that was yours to right what was wrong in the evil administration of this city. You have allowed the poor to be herded together so that one thinks of certain places in Dublin as of a pestilence. There are 20,000 rooms, in each of which are entire families, and sometimes more, where no function of the body can be concealed, and delicacy and modesty are creatures that are stilted ere they are born. The obvious duty of you in regard to these things you might have left undone, and it be imputed to ignorance or forgetfulness; but your collective and conscious action as a class in the present labour dispute has revealed you to the world in so malign an aspect that the mirror must be held up to you, so that you may see yourself as every humane person sees you...

You may succeed in your policy and ensure your own damnation by your victory. The men whose manhood you have broken will loathe you, and will always be brooding and scheming to strike a fresh blow. The children will be taught to curse you. The infant being moulded in the womb will have breathed into its starved body the vitality of hate. It is not they — it is you who are the blind Samsons pulling down the pillars of the social order."

It was a social order that tolerated intolerable slums, that affected the outward piety and display of an ostentatiously Catholic city, yet tolerated a brothel area just behind Sackville Street which was one of the largest and most squalid in Europe: Joyce's "Nighttown", known to Dubliners as "Monto" after its principal street, Montgomery Street (now Foley Street). But the old order was about to be swept away. A few months after the Lockout ended in defeat and Larkin had left for America, Europe's long 99-year peace was broken. In faraway Sarajevo in Austrian Bosnia, Archduke of Austria Franz Ferdinand, heir to the Habsburg throne, was assassinated. By August, the Great War had begun.

Bloom

James Joyce's *Ulysses* is many things, a vast arabesque of a book; a celebration of the ordinary and everyday, written in a manner at times obscure and daunting. It would be wrong to exaggerate this – most of the book is perfectly accessible to any literate adult – but it has been enough to put some readers off. It is their loss. *Ulysses* is the book of life: moreover, it captures the atmosphere of the city in which it is set with an uncanny fidelity. No city – not even Dickens' London – has ever come alive on the page in the way that Dublin does in Joyce's masterpiece.

The narrative of the book is simple enough, albeit the means employed to tell it is not. Stephen Dedalus, the brilliant young intellectual, has left his father's house and is lodging with some student acquaintances. In the course of the day – the entire action is contained less than twenty-four hours – he has breakfast, teaches in a school, wanders on the beach, has a discussion on *Hamlet* with savants in the National Library, goes drinking with medical students and ends up in a brothel.

In the meantime, Leopold Bloom, an advertising salesman, starts his day in his house in Eccles Street. He makes breakfast for his wife Molly, goes about his business (which is conducted at a leisurely pace) in the course of which he meets many people he knows in a city where everyone is known, attends a funeral, has lunch, pops into the National Library at the same time that Stephen is there but does not meet him, briefly visits a pub where he abused by a nationalist fanatic and eventually rescues Stephen from a brawl with soldiers in the brothel area.

This is the climactic moment of the book, the meeting of spiritual father and spiritual son. What follows is really a long coda as they make their way back to Eccles Street where Bloom has offered Stephen shelter for the night. The book ends by switching back to Molly Bloom, already in bed – where she had earlier had an adulterous afternoon with a character called Blazes Boylan – to record her half-awake, half-asleep monologue.

The plot is not the point. The book is told from a series of shifting and highly-elaborated points of view, with a huge cast of minor characters. The celebrated series of internal monologues – more usually referred to as stream of consciousness – allows the reader inside the heads of the principal characters. The action criss-crosses the Edwardian city not just on the day in question – 16 June 1904 – but also recalls past events from the characters' lives, especially those of Bloom and Molly. In Molly's case, this takes us far away from Dublin to Gibraltar where her father, an army officer, had been stationed when she was a girl.

But Dublin is everywhere in the book, like a scent. The locales reach from Dalkey on the far south of the bay to Howth Head at the northern end and take in most of the central part of the Edwardian city as part of the day's action, together with suburbs and nearby mountains in the recollections of various characters. Even with all the changes in the century since the book was set and written, the sense of authenticity – for anyone familiar with Dublin – is uncanny, a point that has been made repeatedly over the years. Its physical descriptions, its capturing of Dublin speech, its miraculous insinuation of the city's atmosphere onto the printed page are such that many people who have never been to Dublin first apprehend the city from *Ulysses* and then discover a familiar place when they eventually arrive in person.

The Reading Room of the National Library of Ireland, a locale less changed than most over the course of time. Chapter 6 of Ulysses *was set in the librarian's office just to the right of the Reading Room.*

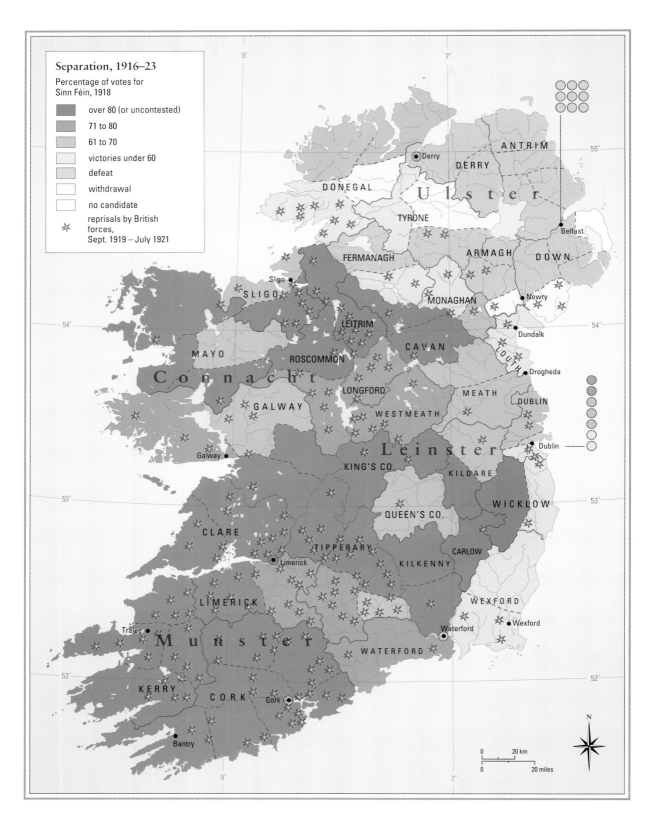

Separation, 1916–23

Percentage of votes for
Sinn Féin, 1918

- over 80 (or uncontested)
- 71 to 80
- 61 to 70
- victories under 60
- defeat
- withdrawal
- no candidate
- ✳ reprisals by British forces, Sept. 1919 – July 1921

Derry

ANTRIM

DERRY

DONEGAL

Ulster

TYRONE

Belfast

FERMANAGH

ARMAGH

DOWN

Sligo

SLIGO

MONAGHAN

Newry

LEITRIM

CAVAN

Dundalk

MAYO

ROSCOMMON

LOUTH

Connacht

LONGFORD

Drogheda

GALWAY

WESTMEATH

MEATH

DUBLIN

Galway

Leinster

Dublin

KING'S CO.

KILDARE

QUEEN'S CO.

WICKLOW

CLARE

TIPPERARY

CARLOW

Limerick

KILKENNY

LIMERICK

WEXFORD

Tralee

Munster

Waterford

Wexford

KERRY

CORK

WATERFORD

Cork

Bantry

N

0   20 km

0   20 miles

CHAPTER 11
CAPITAL

The story of Irish independence – at least for 26 of the 32 counties – has been told so many times that it seems pointless to rehearse it here, except in the most summary fashion. That said, the effect of the events of 1916–22 on the history of the city were transformative.

By 1914, Parnell's successor John Redmond had secured the passage of a Home Rule Act in Westminster. It would have established a devolved Irish government in Dublin, autonomous in domestic affairs but still within the overall structure of the UK. It would not have been a repeal of the Union, but a major amendment to the Union settlement. The measure met adamantine opposition in those parts of Ulster with a Protestant majority, an opposition that proved politically irresistible. That, plus the outbreak of the war, caused the measure to be suspended for the duration.

Famously, the war was supposed to be over by Christmas but instead dragged on for more than four years. By then, Europe was transformed and Ireland with it. A marginal faction of Irish republicans, the most radical and uncompromising of an uncompromising tradition, tripped off a revolt in arms against British rule in Ireland on Easter Monday 1916. Their purpose had been to strike while Britain was at war, on the time-honoured principle that "England's difficulty was Ireland's opportunity".

And so it happened. The rebels occupied a series of public buildings in Dublin and held them for nearly a week. The British government, as surprised as everyone else by this dramatic turn of events, had to divert some troops from the Western Front to combat the rising. It did not scruple to use artillery against rebel positions, of which the principal one – and the most symbolic – was Francis Johnston's General Post Office on Sackville Street. The result was the effective destruction of much of Lower Sackville Street, especially on the north side of the street.

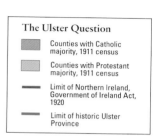

The Ulster Question

- Counties with Catholic majority, 1911 census
- Counties with Protestant majority, 1911 census
- —— Limit of Northern Ireland, Government of Ireland Act, 1920
- —— Limit of historic Ulster Province

The historic Province of Ulster, with the thick red line showing the border created by partition. Although the Province of Northern Ireland thus created had an overall Protestant-Unionist majority, most of the nine counties – and half of the new six-county entity – did not.

Following the rebel surrender, fifteen of the leaders were executed, thus giving the rising its martyrs. The momentum towards a more radical answer to the Irish nationalist question was now increased. Sinn Féin displaced Redmond's Parliamentary Party as the principal nationalist voice. A Treaty was eventually agreed with the British which gave the 26 counties independence outside the UK but not full republican status. This caused a split in republican ranks and a civil war, which the republican radicals opposed to the Treaty lost. However, in an eerie re-run of 1916, they too occupied public buildings in the city and were again routed by artillery, albeit this time fired by their own countrymen.

The principal loss to Dublin was two-fold. The Four Courts was the main republican garrison and it was reduced to a shell by an artillery attack. For historical reasons, it had housed the Public Record Office which held invaluable manuscript sources on Irish history going back to the twelfth century. Before

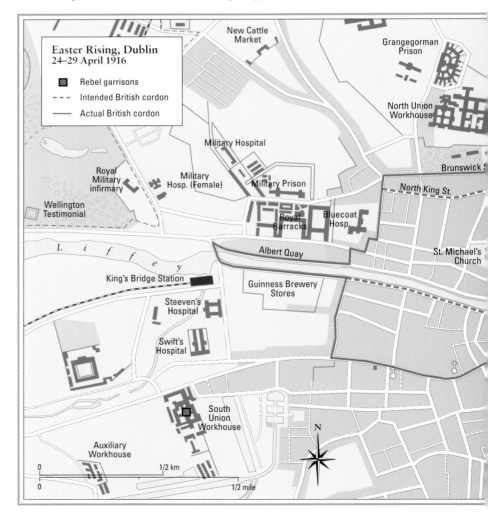

abandoning the building under artillery fire, the republicans set booby-trap bombs for the government forces, one of which exploded and reduced the PRO to ashes. Nor could they plead ignorance: they had been apprised of the cultural and scholarly value of the PRO, but still the super-patriots were content to destroy their country's historical memory.

The other loss was Upper O'Connell Street, as we must now call Sackville following its change of name. Lower O'Connell Street was still in ruins following 1916. Now the upper part of the street, especially on the northern side, was destroyed as government troops displaced the republican forces dug in there.

O'Connell Street had started as an eighteenth-century mall. Then it had mutated into a grand residential street under the eyes of the Wide Street Commissioners. Then gradually, as the nineteenth century wore on, the lower part of the street nearest to the river became more commercial. There was some re-

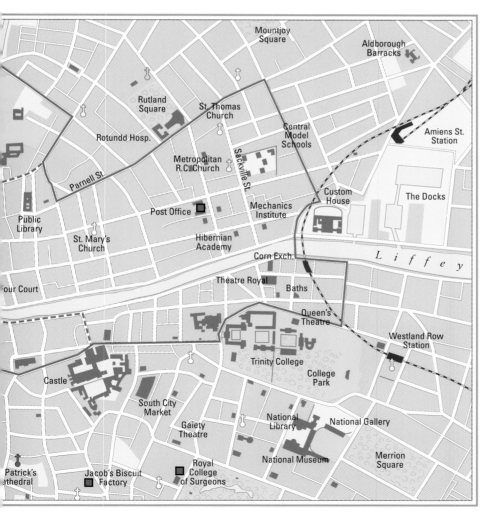

Scenes of destruction in O'Connell Street following the 1916 Rising.

building, most obviously the 1901 Dublin Bread Company building just south of the Abbey Street junction which did not survive 1916. The northern or upper end of the street was less commercial and had lost its way by the end of the century, being neither residentially fashionable any more (with fashion gone south side) while being removed from the commercial and retail centre that stopped at Henry Street.

In *Ulysses*, set in 1904 but written over a decade later, Joyce has Leopold Bloom muse about Upper O'Connell Street as follows:

> "Dead side of the street this. Dull business by day, land agents, temperance hotel, Falconer's railway guide, civil service college, Gill's, Catholic club, the industrious blind. Why? Some reason. Sun or wind."

Bloom was looking at the west side of the street, as the carriage carrying him and his companions in a funeral procession to Glasnevin Cemetery made its way through the city. It was the far side of the street that took the worst punishment during the civil war.

The net effect was that the street had to be almost completely rebuilt. It was fortunate that the city architects of the day, who oversaw the work, were both men of energy and taste. They were C.J. McCarthy and his successor, the wonderfully named Horace Tennyson O'Rourke. Between them, they gave Lower

O'Connell Street, in particular, a pleasing and restrained architectural coherence. The Georgian classicism was gone for good and they resisted any temptation to restore it as pastiche. Instead they substituted a conservative commercial classicism typical of the first quarter of the new century. In Upper O'Connell Street, the restored Gresham Hotel (1927) was designed by the English architect Robert Atkinson. Its discreet neo-classicism, with just a hint of Egyptian decorative themes then in vogue, is particularly successful. Directly across from the Gresham, no. 42 is the last remaining authentically Georgian house in the entire street, an orphan remnant of the glory days.

From 1922, Dublin was a capital again. This time, however, it was no regional centre but the capital city of an independent country. This meant many things, not least a considerable expansion of the bureaucratic infrastructure to reflect the transfer of administrative functions to the new regime. Finance and foreign affairs were the most obvious of these new functions, but the new state was also responsible for education, transport, policing and the legal system, defence, communications and local government. All these powers required the establishment of civil service departments and their staffing. In a poor country, the securing of civil service positions, with their permanent and pensionable security of tenure, became the object of desire for many an ambitious provincial. In the eyes of Dubliners, Cork – now the second city of the new state – was especially fertile in supplying such people, one of whom was memorably described by Oliver St John Gogarty (Joyce's Buck Mulligan) as "a country boy with hair in his ears and hair in his nose and a brief case in his fist".

This influx led in turn to further suburban expansion, with areas being developed on both sides of the river. The inter-war period saw major developments in this regard. It also saw the first serious attempts at substantial slum-clearance projects, in a series of initiatives that did great credit to the governments of independent Ireland, and stood them in a very positive contrast with the old British regime. They were helped by an ideological acceptance of publicly-funded housing schemes that had not existed in Victorian days. The result was that earlier efforts to address the problem of the tenements were worthy but feeble.

The late nineteenth century had seen some successful attempts at private philanthropic initiative to relieve the situation. The establishment of the Dublin Artisans' Dwelling Company in 1876 was one such. It was established by members of the Dublin Sanitary Association, who leased sites from the Corporation that the latter had already acquired and cleared. Their most successful scheme was just off the Coombe in The Liberties, where the sturdy cottages they built still stand in a planned environment that is pleasing to the eye. However, as the company's name suggests, the schemes of the DADC were not aimed at the in-

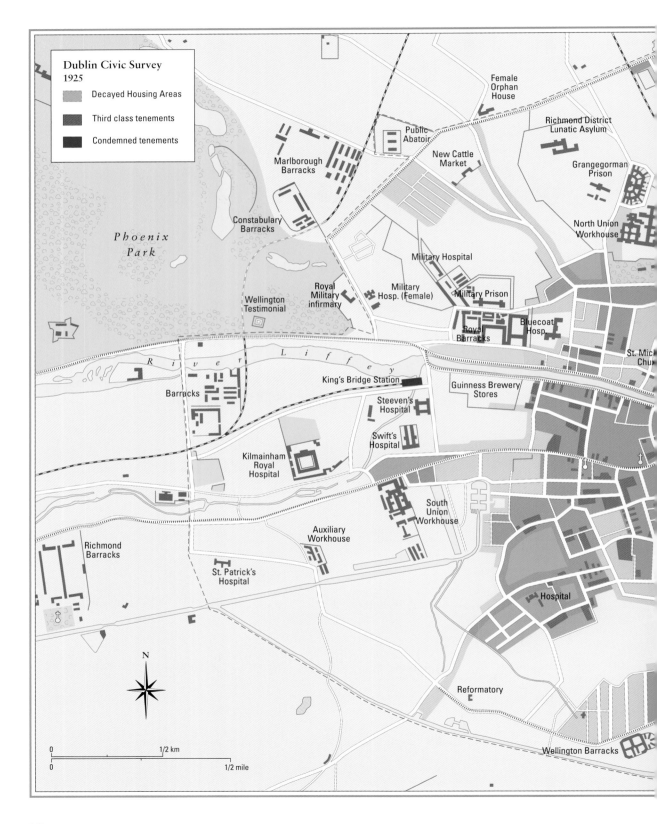

Dublin Civic Survey
1925

Decayed Housing Areas

Third class tenements

Condemned tenements

Female
Orphan
House

Richmond District
Lunatic Asylum

Public
Abatoir

New Cattle
Market

Grangegorman
Prison

Marlborough
Barracks

North Union
Workhouse

Constabulary
Barracks

Military Hospital

Phoenix
Park

Military
Hosp. (Female)

Military Prison

Royal
Military
infirmary

Military
Hosp. (Female)

Bluecoat
Hosp.

Wellington
Testimonial

Royal
Barracks

St. Mic
Chu

R i v e r   L i f f e y

King's Bridge Station

Guinness Brewery
Stores

Barracks

Steeven's
Hospital

Swift's
Hospital

Kilmainham
Royal
Hospital

South
Union
Workhouse

Auxiliary
Workhouse

Richmond
Barracks

St. Patrick's
Hospital

Hospital

N

Reformatory

0   1/2 km

0   1/2 mile

Wellington Barracks

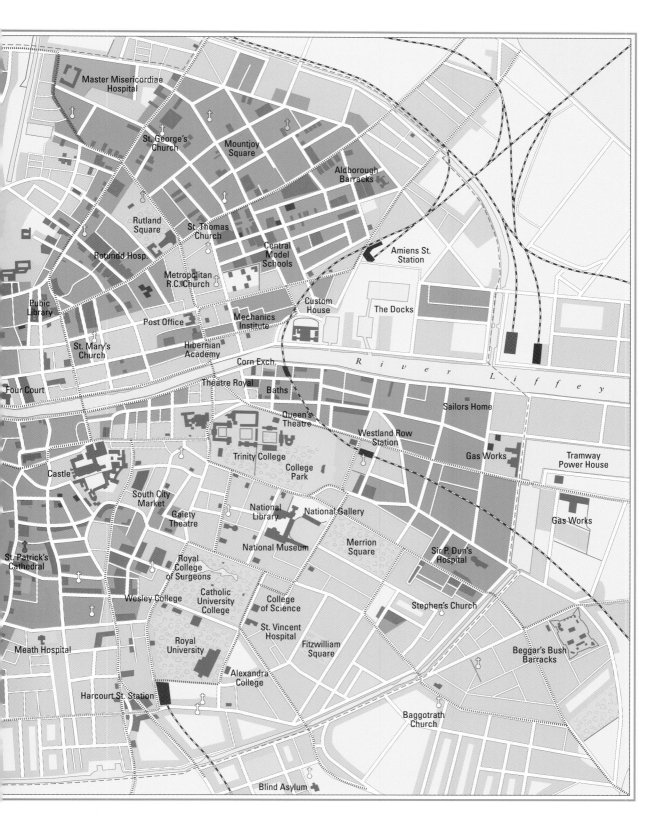

digent poor but at skilled tradesmen and their families. References were required before a tenant could take possession and regular employment in a steady job was a pre-requisite. The company was run as a commercial entity, not as a charity, and was designed to yield a return to its investors. As for the Corporation, the cost of acquiring the Coombe site originally and then clearing it was not recouped by the paltry sum for which it leased it to the DADC, so that it served less as a precedent than as a warning.

The other major Victorian initiative had been the Guinness Trust, established in 1890 by Sir Arthur Edward Guinness who donated £50,000 in trust to alleviate bad housing conditions in the city. This mutated into the Iveagh Trust in 1903. It cleared the area between St Patrick's Cathedral and Werburgh Street, one notorious even by Dublin standards, created St Patrick's Park beside the cathedral and constructed the imposing red-brick apartment buildings in Bull Alley Street and environs.

These initiatives, while successful in themselves, left the greater part of the problem untouched. It was not until the new state took a direct hand in the matter in the 1920s and 1930s that real progress started to be made. The beautifully laid-out Marino estate on the north side was a product of the 1920s. On the south side, Crumlin, bigger than Marino and less successful visually and architecturally, was none the less a blessing for families who had hitherto faced nothing other than exorbitant rents in squalid city centre tenements. Nearby, Drimnagh was also developed as a public housing estate in a similar fashion, as were Cabra and Finglas on the north side. This all meant the commitment of public funds on a lavish scale, an achievement all the more meritorious for the fact that the state was poor.

The effect was that the twentieth century and an independent government managed to resolve the biggest social problem that had defeated the nineteenth-century British administration. Other forces helped, not least Catholic lay organisations like the Legion of Mary, whose Marian ardour was offended by the widespread prostitution in the city and which campaigned successfully to close the Monto town. They saw the overcrowded slums as a breeding ground for vice: a by-product of their zeal was the increased political pressure which the Catholic Church – by now in a position of uncontested moral authority in the country – could bring to bear on government.

The slum clearance schemes reinforced an historic pattern, by emphasising that the west of the city was mainly for the poorer classes and the east for the relatively well-to-do. The majority of the new slum clearance public housing estates were in the west, logically enough since that was where land was most readily available. East was the sea, north was the airport, south were the mountains: the west was easiest. But it reinforced a stark east-west divide that had

A Dublin Corporation suburban housing estate which was typical of the heroic slum clearance efforts between the 1930s and the 1960s.

been growing for 200 years and that now represented the real social demarcation in city life. Much humour is expended on north side-south side jokes and the differences they invoke have psychological reality but the east-west divide is more potent sociologically.

The time from independence to the end of the 1950s is generally regarded as a time of stagnation. One historian titled his book on the period *Preventing the Future* with an even more telling sub-title: *Why Ireland was So Poor for So Long*. Dublin was no exception to the general rule. Emigration – a constant in Irish life since the Famine, continued unabated and reached frightening proportions in the 1950s. Dublin had been by-passed by the Industrial Revolution and remained largely a commercial city with no heavy industry and very few large enterprises, of which Guinness remained the most famous.

Culturally, the new state enjoyed the prestige of seeing two Dublin natives, Yeats and Shaw, receive the Nobel Prize for Literature in the 1920s, and the opening of the Gate Theatre in 1928 brought international drama, presented to the highest professional standards, to the city for the first time. Alas, it was a less happy time at the Abbey. A second major riot greeted Sean O'Casey's *The Plough and the Stars* in 1926, his play set during the Rising ten years earlier.

That, plus the Abbey's rejection of his next offering, *The Silver Tassie*, drove O'Casey into embittered exile in England. The theatre then fell under the management of Ernest Blythe, a narrow-minded ex-politician and Irish-language enthusiast, under whose dead hand it atrophied for a generation.

It was a wretched time for writers given the state's hostile indifference to literature. This was best (or worst) expressed in the fit of rural peasant piety that was the Censorship of Publications Act 1929, which made Ireland a laughing-stock by banning just about every modern novelist of any literary stature. None the less, the city's literary tradition continued to flourish, albeit in difficult circumstances. Even the vast shadow of Yeats, who lived until 1939, could not prevent the emergence of a younger generation of poets, of whom Patrick Kavanagh was the most gifted. His *The Great Hunger* is the most compelling poetic work to emerge from Ireland towards the mid century. His friend Brian O'Nolan/Flann O'Brien/Myles na Gopaleen produced two novels of genius, *At Swim Two Birds* (1939) and *The Third Policeman* (1941/1967), but the rejection of the latter as a result of wartime restrictions disturbed his development as a novelist: the book was eventually published posthumously. In his Myles persona, he developed into what many regarded as the funniest newspaper columnist in the world. His "Cruiskeen Lawn" column in *The Irish Times* was manically exuberant, and contributed significantly to the gradual revival of that newspaper. But alcoholism dulled his talent and he never fulfilled his early promise as a novelist, two late works being feeble by comparison with his brilliant beginning.

No discussion of literature in twentieth-century Dublin can ignore James Joyce's *Ulysses*, published in the year the new state was founded, 1922. Although Joyce had left Dublin in 1904 – the year in which the novel is set – and had only returned for two brief visits in 1909 and 1912, he wrote about the city with an intimacy that has no parallel in literature. Not even Dickens' London feels as real as Joyce's Dublin: the kaleidoscope of urban characters; the uncanny ear for the nuances of Dublin speech and diction; the evocation of the city's atmosphere and personality by a manipulation of language that is masterly and complete. Joyce did not like his native city, his "centre of paralysis" but he presented it with a breathtaking fidelity. Even at the remove of time since composition and publication, anyone with a close knowledge of the city will recognise it from the pages of this masterpiece.

The Eucharistic Congress of 1932 was the great set-piece of the new Catholic ascendancy. A papal legate came from Rome, John McCormack sang for the million-strong congregation at a Mass in the Phoenix Park. A special altar was erected on O'Connell Bridge. All in all, it was an unambiguous statement of Catholic power.

That power was consolidated from 1940 by one of the most remarkable men ever to occupy the position of Archbishop of Dublin, John Charles McQuaid. A rigorist and an ascetic of narrow but acute intelligence, he oversaw a huge expansion of the institutional church in the city. Between 1948 and 1965, he built 34 new churches and 67 secondary schools to serve the expanding suburbs. He established a number of social agencies to give the church a key voice in areas of family support where he had a pathological suspicion of the state. He was instrumental in procuring the dismissal of a left-wing maverick Minister for Health whose Mother and Child Scheme would have provided free medical care for mothers and their children under 16 years of age. This was offensive to McQuaid's belief that the state should not usurp (as he saw it) the proper responsibility of the family in such matters, although he clearly had the church in mind as well. In fact, the archbishop had a distinctly nineteenth-century view of social provision and the role of the state; in many respects he was still fighting the French Revolution.

John Charles McQuaid, Roman Catholic Archbishop of Dublin from 1940 to 1972.

But McQuaid's day was passing. The dismal 1950s, a time of bleak social and economic stagnation and of terrifying levels of emigration, were about to yield to the '60s, when Ireland enjoyed its first period of real economic expansion since the Famine, along with novelties like television, supermarkets and the first shoots of secularism. The high-water mark of Catholic power was past, although few recognised this at the time. The changes that were coming were to further alter the face of the Irish capital. After generations of stagnation, there were going to be some changes made.

Suburb

The first half of the twentieth century was not a time of economic dynamism in Ireland. Quite the contrary: political choices based on protectionism, economic nationalism, and the sub-division of viable, large farms into non-viable smaller units conspired to reduce the country to a state of penury by the end of the 1950s. Over 400,000 people were forced to emigrate in that dismal decade alone, out of a population of less than 3 million as at the census of 1951.

Dublin was no exception to this national rule. Yet in this period, the city experienced an astonishing physical expansion, as a vigorous programme of slum clearance in the decayed centre saw people re-housed in suburban estates, especially on the western fringes.

The huge contiguous public-authority estates of Ballyfermot, Drimnagh and Crumlin, in particular, wrapped around the south-western margin of the city like a girdle. They reinforced an historic trend whereby the west was confirmed as the poorer quarter of the city. This had been so since medieval times. The real sociology of Dublin is not found in the fabled northside-southside split, which is good for jokes and states of mind, but rather in an east-west orientation. East – nearer to the bay – is good. The north-south divide is not entirely a fiction, however. Middle-class private housing pushes farther inland on the south side. On the north side, it is a much thinner membrane.

The creation of large working-class public housing estates at a time of general economic stagnation was a remarkable achievement by the governments of the newly independent state. It addressed squarely the biggest and most intractable problem bequeathed by the Victorian city: what to do about the appalling slums. The houses on the new estates were small but they had modern sanitation and fresh air, in rather pointed contrast to the foetid slums.

Hand in hand with this public provision, there was a corresponding expansion of private suburban housing. This was driven by the development of the building society movement, which advanced mortgage credit for the purchase of houses, many of them sold to a new generation of public servants, originally from the provinces, who now manned the offices of the new state's bureaucracy.

The net effect was a huge physical expansion of the city beyond its previous boundaries, a process that continued in the second half of the twentieth century and has only been halted by the economic tsunami of 2008. The result has been the creation of one of the lowest-density cities in the world: Dublin, with a population similar to that of Copenhagen, sprawls over four times the area of the Danish capital. This makes the development of a coherent public-transport system especially difficult, as all such efficient systems depend upon a minimum density which Dublin does not even begin to approach.

This in turn makes the tyranny of the private car an entirely rational choice for individuals. But it compounds a traffic problem that seems to defy all efforts to correct it. Ad hoc initiatives – dedicated bus lanes and such like – have a sticking plaster effect in the absence of an overall coherent plan.

The dramatic physical growth of the city has been the defining characteristic of twentieth-century Dublin. If the form that it has taken is one of low-density, suburban ribbon development, it is worth recalling that this arose in large part in order to undo a previously disastrous regime of high-density inner-city concentration: the tenement slums. Dubliners of every degree associate individual housing units with front and back gardens as the desired ideal, especially for families with small children. Inner-city apartment dwelling is but weakly developed, although a much greater feature of the city than in the pre-Celtic Tiger years.

New middle-class suburban housing which has been typical of the various building booms since the 1960s.

CHAPTER 12

BOOM, BUST AND BOOM

Writing in the mid '60s, the architectural critic of the *Financial Times*, H.A.N. Brockman, had this to say: "The only reason why Dublin remained for so long the beautiful eighteenth-century city the English built is that the Irish were too poor to pull it down. This, unfortunately, is no longer the case." It was provocative and prophetic all at once. Georgian Dublin, the core of the city, was regarded as either hopelessly derelict or hopelessly passé, or both.

The boom of the 1960s was quite remarkable given the economic history of Ireland since the Famine. It was soon forgotten, as the slump of the 1970s and the locust years that followed seemed to swallow its gains. But while it lasted it produced genuine growth and an increase in household wealth, an end to emigration, the first questioning of the moral monopoly of the Catholic church and an impulse towards modernity. It marked the generational change from the revolutionary to the post-revolutionary. The men who made the revolution were symbolised by Eamon de Valera (1882–1975), who had only stepped down as Taoiseach in 1959 and then assumed the Presidency. The new generation were nearly all born after the foundation of the state, the most glamorous and talented of them being Charles Haughey (1925–2006).

Unlike their stuffy and severe seniors, the new generation were fun. They were making a wave of prosperity and surfing it. Unfortunately, the whiff of corruption was present from the start, especially where Haughey was concerned. He lived an extravagant, aristocratic lifestyle way beyond his visible means. His country house in north Co. Dublin had been built for none other than John Beresford – the onlie begetter of the Custom House – and designed by Gandon. Haughey may not have initiated the growing connection between Fianna Fáil, the almost-permanent government party, and the construction industry, but he symbolised it. From the mid '60s, FF became the builders' party. And Haughey became the builders' kept man, as was eventually discovered in the 1990s when the sources of his "wealth" eventually came to light.

Builders are there to build, and economic booms give them every incentive to do so. The '60s were no exception. The builders and speculators were for the most part from rural backgrounds – a hugely disproportionate number

Opposite: *The Spire of Dublin which had divided public opinion.*

155

from the West of Ireland – and tended to be FF supporters both by inclination and material interest. That meant no love or empathy for Georgian architecture: "the city the English built". It was a sentiment made clear by Kevin Boland, a cabinet minister and scion of a FF family, who stated baldly of two fine Georgian houses in Kildare Street quite needlessly knocked down: "I was glad to see them go. They stood for everything I hate." Both by dint of their provenance and their state of decay, it was a sentiment widely shared.

There was no doubting the decay in what was left of the slums. Places like Dominick Street, originally one of the most magnificent streets in the city, were a shambles by the 1960s. In 1963, in nearby Bolton Street, a Georgian tenement collapsed in the small hours of the morning, killing two elderly occupants. In Fenian Street near Merrion Square, another house collapse ten days later killed two little girls on their way to a shop. It would have required a culture of heroic restoration to revive streets like these. But no one was interested in restoration. True, the Irish Georgian Society had been founded in 1958 by the Hon. Desmond Guinness and his wife Mariga with aim of preserving the country's Georgian architectural heritage, but it was their architecture, not the people's. For the people, or at least those people concerned to develop and build, it could so easily be represented as "everything we hate".

So the decayed Georgian tenement houses were gradually replaced by hideous public-authority flats, while the houses in the better areas of the city – the south-east quadrant for the most part – were targeted for redevelopment. In these areas, the problem was shabby-genteel decline rather than dereliction, but these were places in which developers could turn a profit: there was no prestige or profit to be had in Dominick Street, away over in the long unfashionable north-west of town.

Two developments must stand for the 1960s barbarism, Fitzwilliam Street and Hume Street. In 1964, the state-owned Electricity Supply Board got planning permission to demolish nos 13–28 Lower Fitzwilliam Street, which it owned and wished to replace with a modern office block. The demolition was completed the following year and the office block was duly built and fully opened in 1970. The best that can be said of it is that it could have been worse. It is undistinguished, but at least it maintained the horizontal roof line of what it replaced, so that its effect on what had been the city's longest continuous Georgian vista – from Holles Street hospital to Leeson Street – was less than it otherwise might have been. But it was and still is the wrong building in the wrong place.

Hume Street was slightly different, although the issue was the same. The two houses in question, on the corner of Hume Street and St Stephen's Green, were owned by the state and sold to a developer. Coming in the wake of the Fitzwilliam Street fiasco, it led to an occupation of the site by protesters before it was eventually redeveloped in a deeply unsuccessful and insensitive Georgian-pastiche. The protest was evidence of a changing sensibility as the decade turned into the 1970s, albeit a minority sensibility still. Some of the protesters were architectural students; a few years earlier, at the time of the ESB controversy, architectural students voiced their support for the development, on the shallow but understandable basis that they did not want Dublin to become a museum city. Something had shifted in the intervening years.

Designed by Santiago Calatrava, the James Joyce Bridge was opened in 2003.

The two oil crises of the 1970s and spectacular economic mismanagement by government brought the boom to a shuddering end. From the mid 1970s to the early 1990s, it seemed that the bad old days were back again: the best and the brightest were emigrating in droves. The building boom slowed accordingly, although it was the mid '80s before it really hit the buffers, with the collapse of the property empire of Patrick Gallagher, heir to a family business that had always been very close to Charles Haughey. A month before the banks called in the receiver to the Gallagher empire, Patrick had valued his assets at £60m. A year later, their estimated realisable value was down to £26m. He was not alone. The building craze was over for moment.

There are few major buildings from the twenty-five years following 1960, especially on sensitive sites, that are unqualified successes. Some, such as the hideous Liberty Hall beside the Custom House, are a blot on the landscape. The same can be said for Apollo House and Hawkins House in Poolbeg Street, just on the other side of Butt bridge. To be fair, buildings such as the Central Bank in Dame Street and the headquarters of the Bank of Ireland in Baggot Street have their champions, with some justice. But in general, it was a dismal time for architecture. Dublin – in its mania to appear modern (and turn a buck) – may be said to have hitched a ride on the international style at a time when that style was at a low ebb.

Meanwhile the relentless suburban sprawl went on as the population grew. The demand was not for apartments or any other form of high-density accommodation, but for suburban semi-detached houses with gardens fore and aft. This meant a huge city footprint, as land was acquired for building way out into what had previously been the countryside. This process would falter in the 1980s without ever quite stopping and then roar back to life with a vengeance in the Celtic Tiger years from the mid '90s.

This led to two consequences worth noting, among many. First, it became a licence to print money for holders of agricultural land who could get it re-zoned for building. The landowners thus had a common interest with the developers: they wanted to sell, the developers wanted to buy. The snag was getting the re-zoning through. This was the responsibility of the City Council, many of whose members were induced through bribery to "do the right thing". A cottage industry grew up whereby councillors took the dosh and voted the re-zoning, often against the anguished advice of city planners.

There was deep corruption in the planning process for many years. Bribery was the least of it. The key was a network of builders and politicians who scratched each others' backs. One cabinet minister had an expensive house built for him by builders to whom he was notoriously close and for whom he was believed to have facilitated re-zonings. The revelations that have emerged in a series of tribunals lasting many years are probably no more than the tip of the iceberg. There was simply too much money to be made – and quickly. It was irresistible. But the urban fabric has been the victim of this well-connected private avarice.

The second consequence of low-density suburban sprawl was the near impossibility of running an efficient public transport system to service it. All integrated systems depend on densities far higher than anything Dublin was developing. On top of that, transport policy for the city remained shambolic and chaotic. The trams were abandoned way back in 1949, since when the busses have been the workhorses of the system. The coastal suburban railway – part of

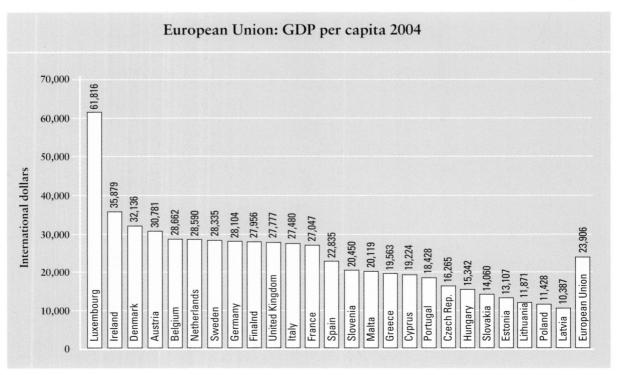

European Union: GDP per capita 2004

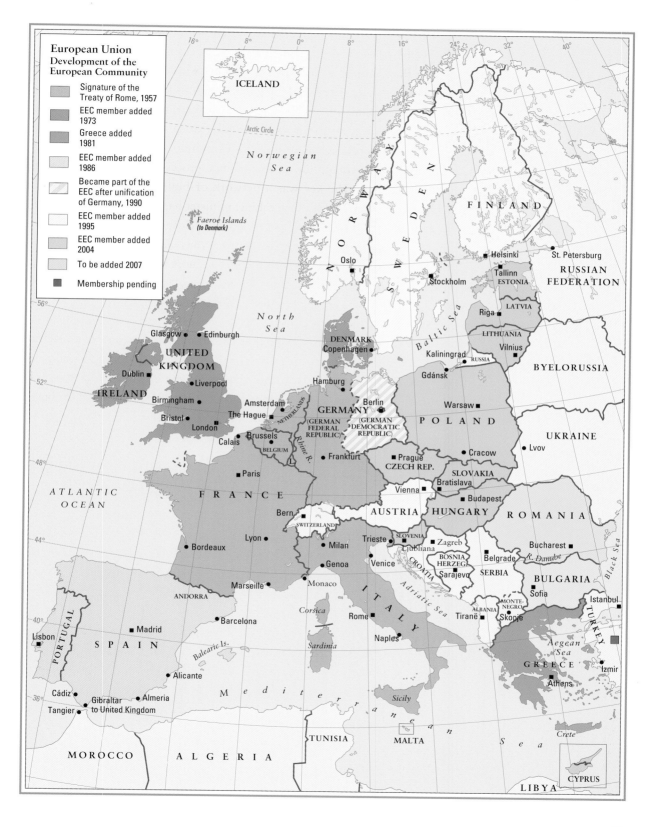

European Union
Development of the European Community

- Signature of the Treaty of Rome, 1957
- EEC member added 1973
- Greece added 1981
- EEC member added 1986
- Became part of the EEC after unification of Germany, 1990
- EEC member added 1995
- EEC member added 2004
- To be added 2007
- Membership pending

ICELAND

Arctic Circle

Norwegian Sea

FINLAND

Helsinki
St. Petersburg
RUSSIAN FEDERATION
Stockholm
Tallinn
ESTONIA
Oslo

Faeroe Islands
(to Denmark)

North Sea

Riga
LATVIA
LITHUANIA
Vilnius

DENMARK
Copenhagen
Kaliningrad
RUSSIA
BYELORUSSIA

Glasgow
Edinburgh
Gdánsk

UNITED KINGDOM
Dublin
Liverpool
Hamburg
Berlin
Warsaw
IRELAND
Birmingham
Amsterdam
NETHERLANDS
GERMANY
(GERMAN FEDERAL REPUBLIC)
(GERMAN DEMOCRATIC REPUBLIC)
POLAND
Bristol
London
The Hague
Brussels
BELGIUM
Rhine R.
Frankfurt
Prague
CZECH REP.
Cracow
UKRAINE
Lvov
Calais

ATLANTIC OCEAN

Paris
FRANCE
Vienna
Bern
AUSTRIA
HUNGARY
Budapest
SLOVAKIA
Bratislava
ROMANIA
Lyon
SWITZERLAND
Milan
Trieste
SLOVENIA
Ljubljana
Zagreb
Bucharest
Bordeaux
Genoa
Venice
CROATIA
BOSNIA HERZEG
Belgrade
R. Danube
Black Sea
Marseille
Monaco
ITALY
Adriatic Sea
Sarajevo
SERBIA
BULGARIA
ANDORRA
Corsica
Rome
ALBANIA
MONTE-NEGRO
Sofia
Istanbul
PORTUGAL
Madrid
Naples
Tiranë
Skopje
TURKEY
Lisbon
SPAIN
Sardinia
Aegean Sea
Barcelona
GREECE
Izmir
Balearic Is.
Alicante
Athens
Cádiz
Almeria
Gibraltar to United Kingdom
Tangier
Mediterranean Sea
Sicily
Crete
MOROCCO
ALGERIA
TUNISIA
MALTA
CYPRUS
LIBYA

the Belfast main line on the north side and the Wexford main line on the south – was electrified in the 1980s and rebranded as the Dublin Area Rapid Transit (DART). It is of course no such thing; it is just a single line and while excellent in itself, links to no other similar line. There is an outer suburban rail system (Arrow) to serve the dormitory towns that exploded in the Celtic Tiger years. And there is the Luas – a modernised tram system, all very nice and well patronised – but it comprises a mere two lines with no interchange between them. To top it all, there is no integrated ticketing between rail, bus and tram systems.

This is a massive political failure over many years. The result is that the modern city is excessively car dependent. Very sensibly, an orbital motorway, the M50, was developed from the late 1980s onwards. It was recommended that it be built three-lanes each way, but a government decision to build only two lanes in order to save money was soon shown to be short-sighted. Before long, even before the Celtic Tiger boom in car ownership was properly under way, the M50 was notorious for traffic congestion. It intersects with all the national primary routes, but the intersections were not free-flowing as is normal international practice, but were in the form of traffic-light controlled roundabouts. This was another penny-pinching expedient. The road is tolled at the West Link bridge and for years a toll plaza, operated by a private company granted a licence by the state, was another notorious congestion spot. To top it all, the state then gave planning permissions to property interests to develop shopping centres and other retail and business parks along the route of the motorway, thus vitiating its function. Instead of being a relief road, it is an access road.

An example of what intelligent planning can achieve is shown in the Temple Bar area, just south of the river. Neglected for years, much of it was owned by CIE, the national transport company, which intended to make it the city's principal transport hub. While waiting to complete its property portfolio in fulfilment of this scheme, it let its existing properties at low rents. This attracted artists and quirky shops to the area. Out of this, an idea was born that the transport plan might be aborted and the area turned into a cultural quarter. This obviously required political muscle, and to his eternal credit it was forthcoming from Charles Haughey, Taoiseach from 1987 to 1992. This fascinating, malevolent, corrupt and charming man established a not-for-profit company to oversee the development of the area.

It has been an almost unqualified success. There is a mixture of residential, retail, restaurants, pubs (too many), theatres and studios and, most of all, an air of energy and even style. It is a model for what could be done elsewhere with greater political imagination and will.

Another Haughey initiative was the International Financial Services Centre on the north quays, which prompted a wholesale redevelopment of the quays on both sides of the river from Talbot Memorial bridge to the East Link. The IFSC drew subsidiaries of major international finance houses to Dublin to participate in the long financial boom that ended only in the crash of 2008. It helped that the IFSC acquired a reputation for slack regulation, even by the standards of an international financial system where light regulation was the prevailing norm. During the boom, the culture of light regulation in the IFSC was either denied or (more plausibly) explained by saying that Ireland was coming from a long way back and needed to buy some competitive advantage. It was great while it lasted; it looks less pretty now.

However, the new buildings at the IFSC are outstandingly successful and are a genuine addition to the city's furniture. A whole residential area, suitably high-density, has grown up right behind it, although at its margins it touches on one of the poorest subsisting areas of old Dublin around Sheriff Street. As in the eighteenth century, new wealth and old poverty can be cheek-by-jowl. Along the river front, a series of handsome if rather unambitious buildings have greatly improved what had been a derelict area. The new National Conference Centre, a dramatic exception to the prevailing caution, is the stand-out building that the area needs.

Temple Bar at night.

Culturally, the city has been enriched since the 1960s. The opening of the National Concert Hall in the '80s in Earlsfort Terrace, on the site of UCD's old Aula Max, filled a gap of long standing. UCD had abandoned the Terrace for suburban Belfield ten years earlier. The removal of a major university from the city centre may have been practical but was culturally dubious. Trinity reclaimed its status as a central city institution, partly as a result of its rival's departure to the suburbs, and partly because a ban on Catholic students studying there was lifted in the 1970s. The ban had been of recent vintage, imposed by John Charles McQuaid and promptly removed by his successor. It reflected an older division: Trinity had traditionally been a Protestant institution and UCD had first developed as a specifically Catholic one. In a sense, the fact that McQuaid felt the necessity to formalise the division by interdict was a sign of weakness, not strength. Under the pressure of developing secularism, many middle-class Catholic students simply ignored the ban.

The first major exhibition of international art in the modern idiom took place in 1967 under the rubric ROSC. Since then, the development of the new Royal Hibernian Gallery in Ely Place and of the Irish Museum of Modern Art in the Royal Hospital Kilmainham have enriched the city's life. The National Museum of Ireland has expanded its holdings and premises under the energetic direction of Dr Patrick Wallace. The Chester Beatty Library, treasures of a private collector, was moved into custom-built premises in Dublin Castle in the 1990s. It is an exceptional collection of Islamic and oriental manuscripts and artefacts, and deservedly one of the major tourist attractions in the city.

It could be argued that Croke Park, the headquarters of the Gaelic Athletic Association on the north side, is the single most impressive structure put up in the city in living memory. It is the fourth-largest sports stadium in Europe by capacity and is an architectural and design triumph.

The city retains its distinct personality. It is not for nothing that Joyce's *Ulysses* still resonates. There is new money glitter and shabby gentility side by side. There is still downright poverty among large numbers of people untouched or little touched by the boom. Even many of

0 1/2 km
0 1/2 mile

Phoenix Park

National Museum at Collins Barracks

Seán Hueston Bridge
Frank Sherwin Bridge
Rory O'More Bridge
James Joyce Bridge
St Michael's Church

Hueston Station

River Liffey

Guinness Brewery

Father Mathew Bridge

IMMA

N

those better off are heavily indebted as a result of borrowing against inflating property values that have now started to tumble again, leaving Ireland with the unenviable record of having the highest rate of personal debt to income in the developed world. The city is vastly more self-assured than it was at the start of the 1960s but, as always, there are anxieties and fears for the future. The collapse in property values has caught many people out. Getting around is an increasing problem given the dysfunctional state of public transport. But the city at its best still retains its peculiar charm: the salty, slightly malicious wit; the old pubs; the view along Merrion Square north to the Peppercannister Church.

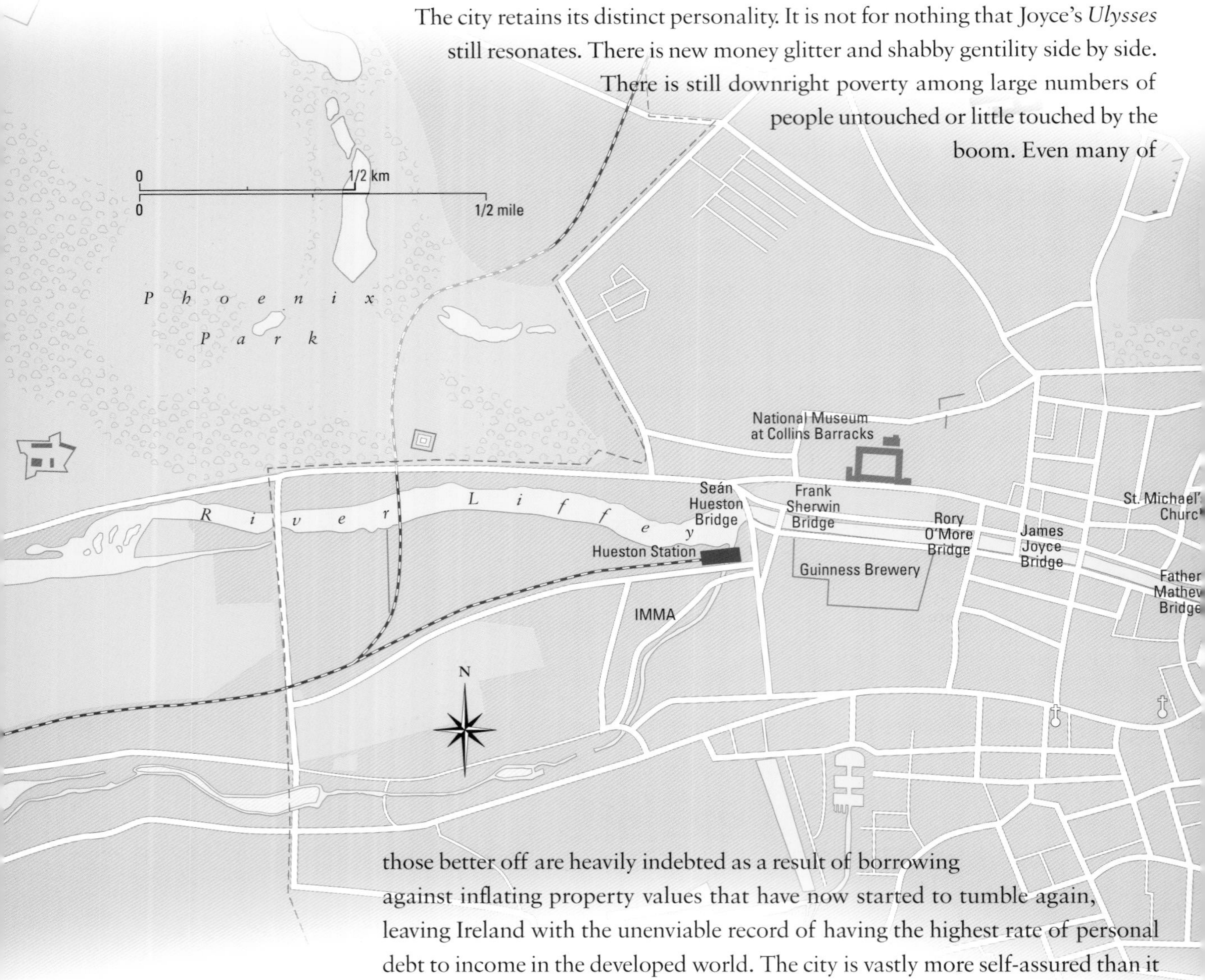

I am a Dubliner and I live here. Perhaps the last word ought to go to a visitor.

The great Dutch journalist and historian Geert Mak travelled all around Europe in 2000, millennium year, and wrote about his experiences and observations in a book that has become something of a modern classic. *In Europe* eventually brings him to Dublin. Here is part of his report:

"Keeping up appearances is a concept completely foreign to Dubliners. They gave up the fight long ago, everyone trundles down the street here in equal disarray…. Quilted vests are the height of fashion here, the women push rusty prams. Even in the Czech Republic, the roads and houses look better

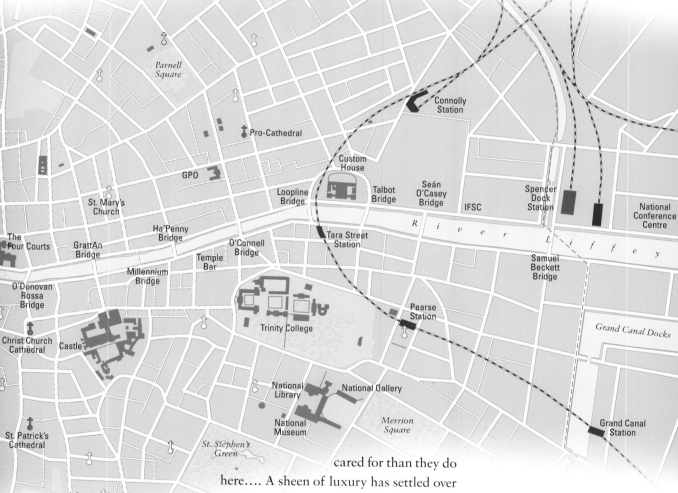

cared for than they do here…. A sheen of luxury has settled over Dublin's shabby city centre… the television shows reports of a fire in a working-class neighbourhood on the edge of town, a complete shambles, two children killed. The camera zooms in on a burned roof, a few cheap pieces of furniture and curtains, toys, a wet street, skinny ladies. No matter what the statistics and the folders say, my eyes see a nation of farmers still marked by the poverty of generations." Discuss.

Cranes crowd Dublin's dockland skyline at the height of the property boom in the early 2000s.

Upland

Travelling through the southern suburb of Rathfarnham and taking the road up hill heading for the Wicklow Mountains brings you in time to a bend in the road between Killashee and Glencree. At this point, you can stop and look back at a stunning panoramic view of the city of Dublin, laid at your feet.

It is all there: the sweeping C of the bay; the enclosing headlands at Dalkey and Howth; the traffic in and out of the port and the ferryport at Dún Laoghaire; in the far northern distance, the airport at Collinstown, now the preferred means of access to the city and departure from it. It is an impressive sight.

It is also a reminder of the nearness of the mountains and of what they have represented historically. Cities of the plain are nervous of the mountains behind them: in Galway, the city gates bore the legend "From the fury of the O'Flahertys O Lord deliver us", the O'Flahertys having been the dominant family in the wilds of nearby Connemara. Likewise, for most of its history, Dublin saw the Wicklow Mountains not as a marvellous leisure upland on the city's doorstep, but as a source of tribal menace.

As early as the 1390s, King Richard II twice brought armies to Ireland to pacify Gaelic families like the O'Byrnes and the Kavanaghs, who raided and despoiled the Pale and constantly threatened Dublin. As mentioned in chapter 4, the citizens made a better fist of pacifying the Wicklow families than the king had done, securing a major victory over them in 1402.

That was by no means the end of it. Until the end of the sixteenth, Wicklow represented a constant threat to Dublin and to the Pale generally. The most famous Gaelic leader of that time was Fiach MacHugh O'Byrne (c.1544–97) who, from his fastness in Glenmalure – in the very heart of the mountains – was a serial raider and plunderer in the Pale. In 1581, the lord deputy himself led a force against O'Byrne, penetrating right into Glenmalure, there to suffer a bloody and humiliating defeat.

Fiach MacHugh O'Byrne is often represented as a sort of proto-nationalist avant la lettre. After all, he harassed the English parts of the country and the English deputy thought enough of him to pursue him to his lair. An anachronistic reading of history, but an understandable one. What seems more to the point is the existential threat that wild, upland regions held for low-lying cities and towns. When this is cross-pollinated with political ambiguity and difference, it makes a potent brew.

Wicklow provided a refuge for rebels in 1798 and again following Emmet's rising in 1803. The military road that carries you past Glencree and towards the

Sally Gap before dropping into Glendalough was built by the British in the wake of these events. Not until the nineteenth century was this hill country completely "tamed" and bent to the bourgeois imperatives of leisure and tourism.

Modern Dublin regards the Wicklow mountains as a lung, a place of exceptional beauty and peace within touching distance of the southern suburbs. So they are. But it was not always thus.

The upper valley of Glenmalure, Co. Wicklow.

SELECT BIBLIOGRAPHY

Barrington, Jonah, *Personal Sketches and Recollections of His Own Time*, Dublin: Ashfield Press 1997

Bennett, Douglas, *Encyclopaedia of Dublin*, Dublin: Gill & Macmillan 1994

Boran, Pat, *A Short History of Dublin*, Cork: Mercier Press 2000

Boylan, Henry, *A Dictionary of Irish Biography*, 3rd ed., Dublin: Gill & Macmillan 1998

Brady, Joseph & Simms, Anngret eds, *Dublin Through Space and Time*, Dublin: Four Courts Press 2001

Clarke, H.B., ed., *Medieval Dublin: the making of a metropolis*, Dublin: Irish Academic Press 1990

Clarke, H.B., ed., *Medieval Dublin: the living city*, Dublin: Irish Academic Press 1990

Clarke, Howard B. ed., *Irish Cities*, Cork: Mercier Press 1995

Clear, Catriona, *Social Change and Everyday Life in Ireland 1850–1922*, Manchester: MUP 2007

Connolly, S.J., *Contested Island: Ireland 1460–1630*, Oxford: OUP 2007

Connolly, S.J. ed., *The Oxford Companion to Irish History*, Oxford: OUP 1998

Craig, Maurice, *Dublin 1660–1860*, Dublin: Allen Figgis 1969

Daly, Mary E., *Dublin, The Deposed Capital: a social and economic history 1860–1914*, Cork: Cork UP 1984

De Courcy, J.W., *The Liffey in Dublin*, Dublin: Gill & Macmillan 1996

Duffy, Sean et al, *Atlas of Irish History*, Dublin: Gill & Macmillan 1997

Fagan, Patrick, *The Second City: portrait of Dublin 1700–1760*, Dublin: Branar 1986

Ferriter, Diarmaid, *The Transformation of Ireland 1900–2000*, London: Profile 2004

Gilligan, H.A., *A History of the Port of Dublin*, Dublin: Gill & Macmillan 1988

Haywood, John, *Historical Atlas of the Vikings*, London: Penguin 1995

Kearns, Kevin, *Dublin Tenement Life: an oral history*, Dublin: Gill & Macmillan 1994

Kilfeather, Siobhán, *Dublin: a cultural and literary history*, Dublin: Liffey Press 2005

Luckett, Richard, *Handel's Messiah: a celebration*, London: Gollancz 1992

Lydon, James, *The Making of Ireland: from ancient times to the present*, London: Routledge 1998

McDonald, Frank, *The Destruction of Dublin*, Dublin: Gill & Macmillan1985

Maxwell, Constantia, *Dublin Under the Georges*, London: Harrap 1946

Milne, Kenneth ed., *Christ Church Cathedral: a history*, Dublin: Four Courts Press 2000

O'Brien, Joseph V., *Dear Dirty Dublin: a city in distress 1899–1916*, London: University of California Press 1982

O'Donnell, E.E., *The Annals of Dublin's Fair City*, Dublin: Wolfhound Press 1987

Pearson, Peter, *The Heart of Dublin: resurgence of an historic city*, Dublin: O'Brien Press 2000

Townshend, Charles, *Easter 1916: the Irish Rebellion*, London: Allen Lane 2005

Welch, Robert ed., *The Oxford Companion to Irish Literature*, Oxford: OUP 1996

INDEX

References in this index in **bold** face are maps and in *italic* face are illustrations. References to monarchs denote Kings/Queens of England/Britain unless otherwise specified.

List of Maps

ACKNOWLEDGEMENTS

The publishers would like to thank the following:

Alamy   11, 93, 129, 154
Imagefile   15, 153, 167
Private Collection   25, 33, 53, 54, 55, 94–95, 115
Red Lion   26, 35, 75, 87,
Sportsfile   29
Dublin City Council   34
Mary Evans   39
Topfoto   43
Peter Newark Historical Pictures   45, 57, 61, 102/103,
National Library of Ireland   47, 65, 72–73 (bottom), 73 (top), 74, 77, 78–79, 80, 83, 97, 111, 113, 117, 120, 139
Linzi Simpson   49 (top), 59, 81
National Museum of Ireland   49 (bottom), 62,
National Gallery of Ireland   51, 88, 123, 139
Private Collection   67
Ashmolean Museum   69
Irish Times   85
Gill & Macmillan   92
Guinness   99
Bridgeman   100
Leeds City Art Gallery   109
Getty   126, 161
Corbis   135, 144
RTE Stills Library   149
Collins Photo   151

Illustrations: Peter A.B. Smith

Cartography and Design: Jeanne Radford, Alexander Swanston, Malcolm Swanston and Jonathan Young for Red Lion Media, Derby, England